YOU'RE NOT INFERTILE.
YOU'RE JUST NOT IN
TIMING.

YOU'RE NOT INFERTILE. YOU'RE JUST NOT IN TIMING.

SUPER NATURAL STRATEGIES TO ACTIVATE YOUR FAITH IN FERTILITY FOR EVERY AREA OF YOUR LIFE.

PORSHEA WILKINS

Porshea Wilkins Ministries

Contents

DEDICATION		vii
FOREWARD		1
INTRODUCTION		3
1	GENERATIONAL BAGGAGE	7
2	MYOMECTOMY AND MINISTRY	21
3	CLOMID AND FIBROIDS	30
4	CLEANING HOUSE	39
5	PROPHETIC ENCOUNTERS	42
6	TIME TO POST UP	57
7	FAITH ACTIVATION	64
8	I DON'T SEE ANYTHING	74
9	PROMISE KEPT	95
10	EAR PLUGS	114
11	THE STRATEGY	121
12	THE SUPERNATURAL	145
REFERENCES		161

About The Author	164
Supernatural Pregnancy Docuseries	165
Docuseries Reviews	167
Midwife Moments Podcast	169

To my Father in Heaven - with tears rolling down my face, I can't say thank you enough. To my beloved husband Nnamdi Jarrod Wilkins-Agomo - you have given me the greatest expression of love you could ever give, your man-man, my stinka-man, our promised baby boy. To my handsome son Aiden Nkwachi - we did it baby boy! I love you beyond every breath in my body. You are forever my Awesome Aiden! I'm so grateful to be your Supernatural Mommy! To my Big Girl Princess Chandler - you have my whole heart! Thank you for making me a mommy first and being the best big sister ever! To every supporter - may Elohim bless you beyond your wildest imaginations. To every woman in waiting - no matter where you are in your journey know this: God is faithful.

Copyright © 2021 by Porshea Wilkins

All rights reserved. No part of this book may be reproduced in any manner whatsoever without written permission except in the case of brief quotations embodied in critical articles and reviews.

First Printing, 2021

FOREWARD

Like many of you, one night as I laid across the couch doing my nightly scroll through Instagram, I found myself intrigued by Porshea's "Supernatural Pregnancy" docuseries. Before I knew it, I was fully engulfed, going to her website to watch every episode. I was blessed by her testimony, to not give up on birthing the promise that God put in your heart be it a baby, a marriage, a career goal; if God placed the desire in you, He will bring it to pass. I immediately sent her a DM, "Amazing!!!! I'm not believing God for a baby, but I am believing God for something big in my personal life. Your story encouraged my faith to keep standing….it shall come to pass!" After a couple of messages back and forth, she said "let's do lunch". What I thought would be a great meeting of two women chatting over a nice meal turned into a real-life Mary and Elizabeth moment.

Porshea and I have known of each other over the years being in the same city, but a mutual family friend caused our paths to cross once again but this time it was different, it was a divine connection. At lunch, with sunlight peeking in through the glass windows, she began to share more about her journey with infertility, marrying her husband, the calling on her life and we sat for hours sharing vision. When she told me the title of her book, "You're Not Infertile, You're Just Not in Timing" the fine hairs on my arms stood and my spirit leaped. It was a confirming word that jolted me. It was the reminder that we are not what society labels as broken, inadequate, nor incomplete we are just in process until the perfect timing of the Lord.

God's timing is everything! For every promise, principle, and prophecy there is a faith process to bring it to pass. Often in the process, we allow doubt and the voice of naysayers to give us a false narrative about who we are. If we are not careful, we will take what they say and allow it to override what God said. If God said it, that settles it! While you wait in faith for the promise to manifest it is critical that you surround yourself with the right people who will not misdiagnose you or try to get you to give up on what God said. You need a midwife, an Elizabeth, a coach, a living example who has walked this road ahead of you. Porshea is the midwife, coach, who so transparently and eloquently shares her testimony so you can be encouraged on your journey. She is a living example sent to focus you so that you can clearly see the supernatural manifest in your life.

You are not what the last pregnancy test said about you. You are not what the last "no" sounded like in your ear. You are not your last failed relationship. You are God's child, and He wants to see you have everything promised to you in His word. Trust the timing and treasure the testimony of others until you see God's promises manifest in your life. This book will take you through Porshea's story but also divine strategy to help you along your journey. From faith confessions, to speaking to your baby, to birthing your baby. "You're Not Infertile, You're Just Not in Timing" is sure to be a reference book for this next season of your life. Written with truth and love, it is a must-read. So, as you journey, give grace to yourself, and brace yourself for the supernatural that is about to overtake you.

Dr. Irishea Hilliard, Ph.D.
Senior Pastor, New Light Church

INTRODUCTION

When I say I had a supernatural pregnancy by God giving me a miracle baby boy many women ask how. Their anticipation for what I will say next lets me know they have been searching for ways to have one themselves; looking for the secret. After five years of trying, overcoming painful medical procedures and countless emotional setbacks, I wholeheartedly understand how it feels to be told you're infertile. God took me on a journey that only He could orchestrate. I just yielded and shared with a trusted few. He told me to document it, and the results of that are what you see today in this book as well as my Supernatural Pregnancy Docuseries. It took longer than I wanted it to and hurt more than anything I could have imagined. There were many days I'd sit and wonder why, many nights I'd cry, weeks I didn't want to show my face and many months where I didn't know if I was coming or going. The process tested every part of my mind, body and soul. My marriage, my family, my finances, my business, and my health all in hospice together. I couldn't see my way through. Life felt like I was driving on a dark road during a foggy winter storm, in a car with broken windows and no headlights. Pitch black would've felt like sunshine.

I'd visit this road many times over the years. Then God would send someone to help with the light through a prophetic word, social media post, phone call, visit or text. All random to me, but intentional to Him. The more I looked for light, the more someone would bring. They never brought me a blanket, tow truck or seemed to have a car of their own to help me with the obvious, they just showed up to my car with some light. The more positive my thoughts, the more light they'd bring. When I realized I determined the amount of light I have, I began to participate more through prayer, fasting and being intentional with my thoughts. I'd cast down and speak away the negative thoughts and words, replacing them with something positive. God told me *"You will eat what you teach"* and the more the light shined the more I could see what was on my plate. I didn't like what I saw. God knew I was hungry, but He let me chose my diet, and since I had the power to choose, I changed the menu. Each time I chose to eat faith versus fear or belief versus doubt the light on that dark road got brighter. The small lights turned into day light. When I looked up, I saw the sun. Next to it a clock. I kept getting negative pregnancy tests so the time on the clock was blurry, but I kept my faith diet. It got warmer outside. I even replaced the broken window on my car door. The path on the road in front of me was clear. I could see grass and trees again. The clouds were so beautiful.

As I drove and kept feeding my spirit the right things the clock began to slowly drop from the sky. With each drop the time on the clock got clearer. It was different from the time on my watch and anytime I'd look at my watch the numbers would shrink on it. Eventually they got too small for me to see, giving me no choice but to focus on the time on the clock in front of me. Once I focused I realized I was driving in the middle of a two-lane highway balanced on both sides, in complete alignment with Gods' time. The closer I got to the clock the more I could hear it wasn't ticking like a normal clock, it was cooing like a little baby. Aiden, my promised baby boy, was inside the clock inspiring me to keep my balance, and stay in alignment. I threw my watch out, pulled up to the clock, got out my car and stepped inside the clock to a nursery so beautiful it could only have come from Heaven. I grabbed my son, sat in a rocking chair and listened to his coos until we both fell asleep, right inside of Gods time.

The baby is literal and metaphoric. For you it could be a child, book, business, marriage, family, healing or whatever it is God promised you. The supernatural strategies I share will apply. The journey God took me on impacted every area of my life. Soon as one area was under control another went crazy. I was juggling in the spirit. The Bible says in **Psalms 37:4 He shall give you the *desires* of your heart.** It's plural because its plentiful. There is no lack in the Kingdom of Heaven. We're not one dimensional.

Everyone in the world says to think outside of the box, and while we're citizens of a country on earth, our home country is Heaven. There is no box at home, according to **Matthew 16:19** only keys that unlock doors of purpose and promise, so while I waited for the implantation of my son in my uterus naturally, I was having contractions in the spirit for so many other areas. Life doesn't stop just because you want to have a baby. You still have to be the what and who you've always been, so infertility looks different for everyone. Whether you're infertile in the womb and have been told you can't have children, infertile in your finances and can't pay your bills, infertile in your relationships and can't keep a man or attract a husband, infertile in your family and can't keep your children in order or family members out your business or infertile in the mind and you can't seem to find peace, I have good news. The Lord told me healing and deliverance will take place for you right where you are, just by watching my Supernatural Pregnancy Docuseries and reading this book. I believe Him. It's birthing season and it's metaphoric. Faith activation will occur for you in so many areas of your life. Your baby is ready in Heaven. The clock is ticking. Prepare to push.

I love you and I'm here.

Porshea Wilkins
Purpose Midwife | Author | Entrepreneur

Chapter 1

GENERATIONAL BAGGAGE

Growing up Black you're told to keep your business in your house. *"What happens in this house stays in this house"* they'd say. While I understand and appreciate the love and protection my elders were speaking from, they unknowingly created a culture of silent suffering. You could be deathly ill, but instead of seeking proper help mentally and psychologically you'd suppress. No one would know what was going on in your home, not even other family members. Thankfully times have changed, but unfortunately black women born in the 80's and sooner find it hard to let go of what's inside. This has left us to carry a tremendous amount of baggage from miscarriages, abortions, endometriosis, fibroids, cervical cancer, IVF, ectopic pregnancies, and more leaking like a heavy period into our careers and everything else, staining our mental health. Imagine generations of women suffering from issues that could help others prevent or prepare and no one is talking about it. In my case I found out I had Fibroids in 2014 after trying to get pregnant with my Husband. I stopped taking my birth control pills and wanted to get a check up to make sure all was well. So, I went to Planned Parenthood for my normal annual pap smear and the results came back abnormal. She felt something foreign when checking my uterus with her hand and said I needed to go to a Gynecologist. After a few months of procrastinating out of fear I found a doctor online and went to see her. After getting my ultrasound results, she tells me I have eight fibroids a mix between grapefruit and almond sized and she'd have to remove them through surgery. I was terrified and felt completely isolated. *What were they? How did I get them? Were they sexually transmitted? Was it something I ate? Were they hereditary? Is surgery the only option? What if something goes wrong? What if they're cancerous? What if I can't have children?*

After having a conversation with my mother, she shared with me that my aunt had them and so did she. Both ended in hysterectomies. I was blown away and even more scared. I knew they'd both had hysterectomies but I didn't know fibroids played a role in it. I also didn't know that they are as common as they are in black women.

> "Studies show that African-American women suffer fibroids 2 to 3 times more than white women," says McLeod OB/GYN Dr. Monica Ploetzke. "We also know that Black women tend to experience fibroids at a younger age and often more severely than their white counterparts." One estimate is that 25% of African-American women will suffer from fibroids by the age of 25 and 80% will have them by age 50 (compared with 70% for white females). Because Black women suffer fibroids at an earlier age, they also are 2 to 3 times more likely to undergo surgery."

I remember feeling small and wanting to hide. I wanted to keep it to myself because I didn't know how I got them or why.

I didn't want to be judged or ridiculed. No one in my circle or community was talking about it publicly so it must be something I did. My Husband was my go-to person for everything, but he was just as taken back as I was. He didn't know how to handle or help me with it, there weren't any women in his life emotionally connected enough for him to automatically know how to step into that role for me, especially since it was about woman stuff. So, he did what most alpha men do in times they have no control or can't solve the problem, he disconnected. His job was to protect me, and he couldn't. He felt helpless. He also desperately wanted a son, and now he's presented with the thought that it may not happen because of my baggage that he now has to carry.

I was hurt, but couldn't blame him for feeling that way. I also knew the feeling of dealing with baggage you had nothing to do with. Many women dream of marriage and kids. My daydreams growing up were about career success. Marriage and kids for me was far down the road, if at all, I really didn't care. At 23, one year after graduating College with a BBA in Marketing, I relocated to Columbus, Ohio from Houston, Texas to be a Brand Manager for an $8 Billion retail lingerie company to manage a $1.4 Billion collection for them. I'd been in retail since my junior year in high school. I beat over 3,000 applicants for that position. I was the only person from Texas and only black person male or female to accomplish it. I was one of two black brand managers in the company. The other woman was a Vice President. I had been speaking that career into existence since high school. While working there I was exposed to so much; private planes and jet trips were monthly, designer labels and exotic cars were the norm and I'd get invited to lavish holiday parties at private estates. It was eye opening being surrounded by so many women living like that. What wasn't appeasing was how their kids were calling the nanny mommy. They had the stuff, title and office with view but not the time to enjoy it. I wanted more and I knew in order to get it I needed to be a boss versus having one, so I started my journey into serial entrepreneurship and moved back to Houston. I was as a motivational speaker for high school and colleges, joined a network marketing company, and did consulting for retail businesses in the Houston area including a shopping mall. Things got very tough financially, but I was always self-sufficient. I negotiated extensions for my car payment, I didn't pay for nine months and they never repossessed it. I lived with an ex-boyfriend from college for a few months while in between gigs, rented a room in the home of a stranger I met online, then got a sales job for a new home builder and moved into my own place. I left that job because it cost more to get there in tolls and gas than I was making on my draw against commissions which required a level of patience and maturity I just didn't have at the time.

I hit the wall again with the 2008 recession and lost all my speaking contracts for high schools and colleges. I heard about this new thing called payday loans, and began to leverage them to float me through the months. I had four in rotation using one to pay the other. It was tough and I don't recommend anyone do the same. My best friend even stepped in to help after her divorce and paid my rent one month. By this time its 2009 when I joined Jarrod in business. When we initially met in 2008 a mutual associate of ours introduced us since we were both public speakers. We learned that we'd both been in the same network marketing company on the same team in 2005 but didn't know each other and agreed to stay in touch. Both of us were broke; he didn't have $150 to pay his light bill and I was facing eviction and repossession, but we were both very driven and focused to change that. I built my network marketing business as a single woman, replaced my corporate income, paid off some of the payday loans I'd gotten, and was on my way to whatever God had for me next. I've never been afraid to do something new and could care less about others' opinions. If I liked it, I was going to go for it. If it didn't work, great! I'd just take what I learned to apply to the next thing.

Needless to say, my plans of becoming who I knew in my heart I was, were too big to include getting pregnant or caring for a baby. His daughter was 10 months when we began working together in 2009, I'd even spend time with her and babysit. Things were strictly platonic between Jarrod and I, he never flirted or made a pass at me, then we became best friends. My relationship with my father was strained at the time, and Jarrod and I were so close I saw him giving me away at my wedding one day. So, I was very taken back when he professed his love for me in May of 2010. He'd sent me a poem and began calling me his rib like in the book of Genesis in the Bible. When I'd pick up the phone to answer his call, he'd day *"Can I speak to my Rib please?"* This man respected me, was driven, caring, focused, chocolate, handsome, knew the Lord and was using the Word of God to court me? I was hooked! He said he knew from the moment he saw my profile picture on Facebook that I was his wife, it was from a wedding I was in a couple of years before. I was so shocked by his love confession I ignored him for a week! The company we were a part of had strict rules for upline/downline relationships. I knew I'd have to shift my focus from my business and eventually give it up because while we knew how to function with him as my coach in business, that wouldn't transfer to a romantic relationship. Plus, he was still engaged.

I knew he dreaded the thought or marrying her, he told me he only proposed because she got pregnant, and he didn't want to disappoint his family. He was eight years younger than her and didn't care for the free spirit anything goes kind of lifestyle she was attracted to. His family told him when he first introduced her that she wasn't the one for him, but he didn't listen. He was still carrying baggage from them abandoning him in Nigeria. His mother took him there when he was five years old to meet his grandmother, gave him a kiss on his forehead and disappeared until she picked him up at age eleven. His grandmother told her that was the only way she'd succeed in Law School. During that time, he suffered physical abuse from his uncle who was released from prison. When his mother finally did come back to get him, he returned to the U.S. where he learned he wasn't the only child anymore and had a younger sister. His parents never married and his mother married someone else, later having another boy and girl. He relived the same culture shock he had when she left him in Nigeria, so anything they had to say about who he should or should not date, went in one ear and out the other. As far as he was concerned, they didn't care about him.

Most Nigerians I know are very strict and direct when it comes to keeping customs and traditions, having a child out of wedlock when you have three younger siblings to set the example for is a disgrace. Doing it with someone they never wanted you with in the first place is a disaster. This is on the heels of dropping out of college to pursue business and everyone in the family is loaded with MBA and PhD's in the medical and criminal justice fields. Both of his parents are successful Attorney's. He disconnected from his Nigerian side for years due to the judgement, I met him during that time of disconnection.

Clearly, I had a lot to process, but I wasn't really worried about the family drama since I had plenty of my own. My dad has three brothers, all Texas raised blue-collar men, hardworking country boys, with high school diplomas, a flask of alcohol, mouth full of snuff, women in rotation, fish in the back yard tank, BBQ on the grill, sitting under a shade tree with a dominoes table and vocabulary loaded with every curse word you can imagine. I was the first to get a college degree on my dad's side. My mother's side is the exact opposite. All degreed up and white collar. She had five siblings, four girls and one boy who was shot in the head and killed by a friend during his visit home from the military.

By saying yes to dating him I'd be saying yes to being a mother to his daughter and supporting him through all the child support court and visitation drama we knew would follow for years. I didn't have relationship baggage but I had financial baggage. I also had emotional baggage from a toxic relationship with father figures; my parents divorced when I was five, my dad was physically and verbally abusive to my mother and very aggressively verbally with me once I got to middle school which was crushing. My mom remarried after a three-week courting period to a man from Louisiana who molested me in high school; so, I had a lot of psychological baggage which created a love hate relationship with my ability to let go of things and people. I call it the gift of goodbye.

Back then, I didn't manage it well and would cut people off and move on with no explanation or thoughts of reconciliation. Now, I understand how to create levels with it through grace. Instead of everyone being cut off immediately forever, they go into one of three categories.

1. Love them alone category. This is where I give space and time for all to heal, including myself. Keeps emotions in check and allows God to work on my heart just as much as theirs so I remain open for Him to reconnect, if it's His will.
2. No access category. This is mostly applied to those whom I am in business with or family. It's a connection you really can't get rid of permanently. I'm cordial enough to get through the time when I see them, keeping the conversation surface, giving no access to anything personal in my life.
3. Gift of goodbye. This is for a repeat offender who failed during the previous categories and I have to remove from

my physical and mental space completely. I always lean on Titus 3:10-11 *for this after a first and second warning reject a divisive man [who promotes heresy and causes dissension—ban him from your fellowship and have nothing more to do with him], 11 well aware that such a person is twisted and is sinning; he is convicted and self-condemned [and is gratified by causing confusion among believers].*

The key for me over the years was finding a healthy way to manage the categories and not jump the gun by putting someone in one area due to my offense about something that wasn't warranted.

After Nnamdi professed his love for me, I ignored him for a week to think everything through, I just knew in my Spirit this would be a very long-term and potentially lifetime commitment. I understood he needed time to transition away from living with his daughter and move into his own place, knowing he wouldn't see her everyday was heart-breaking for him. He knew he could no longer stay in a toxic relationship and be the best Father or person in general. Who he wanted to become required someone with the same values; he's a Kingdom man who loves God, very traditional with a powerful anointing, there's a specific type of woman he needed by his side to carry his vision, and he didn't see it possible in that particular relationship. He officially ended the engagement on July 4, 2010. He called it his personal Independence Day. I'd already done enough of the live-in boyfriend; in the south we call it shacking, and he was tired of it as well, so we began looking for him a place.

The Salt Covenant

Even though we lived separately, every time he had his daughter they stayed at my apartment. I bought her clothes, did her hair, fed her, read to her, had bible study with her, organized all the play dates and activities for her, drive the hour drive one way to pick up or drop her off at school, all the things I'd normally do, because its who I am. Loving her as my own was easy to do, she was the sweetest baby. I'd been in the middle of a parental split before and I didn't want her to feel the weight of it like I did. I focused on making her transition as smooth and loving as possible on our end. My small bedroom was half mine, half hers. God revealed to me His purpose for me in her life, and I went all in in like I would with anything else.

We were becoming a family. This sent a big shock to my family. They knew how serious I was about my goals. I struggled with my identity many times in our relationship, so when the family court and normal drama began with him, I also disconnected. I had many arguments with Jesus about it too. Like, *how did I end up here? This is exactly what I told you I didn't want.* All He kept saying was "*there's purpose here daughter*". After three years I was exhausted and felt stagnant with him. We weren't even engaged yet and his daughter out of the blue began calling me Mommy.

I'm cooking, praying, sitting in court, cleaning, building the business, having sex, everything. I was a whole wife with nothing to show for it! Thankfully we had begun premarital counseling with our Pastor at the time, we didn't want to wait until we were engaged to start, we wanted to get equipped before getting engaged so we'd know if we even wanted to take it that far. He helped Jarrod understand why I was so frustrated when he didn't have a date in mind for an engagement. He reminded him that I know him to be a planful person. Everything that's important to him goes into his calendar; all meetings, events, conference calls, travel etc... he was telling me he wanted me to be his wife, but there was nothing on the calendar metaphoric or otherwise for a proposal. He told him I didn't want to be a volunteer. I told him if I don't get a date then I'm ending the relationship and we can just go back to being friends and business partners. We never had any challenges with those roles. By that time the new relationship fire phase was long gone and we'd seen the worse of each other. It was too much to carry for free and I wasn't willing to do it out of love any longer. He told me often that he doesn't see a life without me in it. At first, I was flattered, but after all this time and drama not anymore. He agreed it was time to take the next step. Our Pastor told him not to give me the exact date so it could be a surprise but I did need to know the month. He told me he will propose by September 30th. I already had my ring on my dream board in my bedroom so he knew what I wanted. We'd even gone to a few jewelers over the years to try on rings and I found the one I wanted.

September 2013 comes and I just knew he'd wait until 11:59pm on September 30th right before the month ended to propose, but he didn't. We got engaged September 5, 2013 while on a business trip at the St. Regis Bal Harbor in Miami. He proposed on the beach, and with the help of a business partner, led me down to the shore where there were white beds covered in flowers, and a message to me written in the sand, *"Porshea today is your day. Will you be my wife."* By the time I finished reading he was down on one knee in front of me. The rest was a blur, I just remember weeping with my face in his chest. We didn't want or need a long engagement, so we set our wedding date for six months later, March 1, 2014.

Our leases were about to be up on our apartments, so we began looking for houses with move-in dates around that time to move in as Husband and Wife. We found a new construction home that was just finished in December 2013 in a beautiful newly developing suburb. The moment I walked in and saw the kitchen island I knew it was ours. We signed the lease on January 30th, he moved in first, then I followed in February. We had our wedding there as well, a barefoot ceremony in the living room, wearing a suit and dress out of our closet. I prepared the menu and cooked all the food by myself the night before. That was my dream, I didn't want a fancy dress and all the normal bells, whistles, and expense of a wedding. It never made sense to me to spend thousands of dollars on a wedding, and have a two-dollar marriage. We were intentional with our three year courtship, and invested so much time developing the marriage that the wedding was more for a formality.

I just wanted my kitchen island to be set up like the Barefoot Contessa's on the Food Network. I'd been watching her for years! Our daughter was five by then and couldn't wait for the big day. All she wanted was to call me Mommy, have her own room in a house with stairs and a little brother. Even though she started calling me mommy at age two, we told her to wait until we were married so Jesus can have his blessing on it. We wanted to set a Godly example. We told her after we get married, she can call me either Mommy or Mama P it's her choice. She'd yell in her cute little voice with a big grin on her face, *I'm going to call you MOMMY!!* Then she'd dive in my arms for big hug and kiss. Nearly every day she was with us she'd ask over and over when were *we* getting married, she thought she was going to get married to us too. So innocent and cute. We never gave her a date because we didn't want any interference, so we just told her very soon. To keep her mind off of the date I told her we wanted her to open the wedding up with the Lord's prayer. Her little eyes got so big with excitement. The plan we gave her was to say it every night before bed so she would know it well enough to recite it in front of everyone including our Pastor at the time. She took her role so serious and practiced everyday she was with us, even while watching Mickey Mouse Clubhouse or Dora the Explorer, I'd see her mumbling it. She's my Big Girl Princess for sure. I began to amplify teaching her the Word of God. She'd fall asleep listening to sermons from Dr. Myles Munroe, Bishop TD Jakes and other Pastors at bedtime. I bought her a couple of kids bibles to read. Her assignment would be to read five to ten pages and write a summary each morning. We'd then discuss it during breakfast or on the drive to school. She was always very animated in her analogies of everything. I remember one day when we were in church, she sat in the sanctuary with us and it was a heavy move of God. We were all told to stand up and get in a circle of two or three people and recite what the Pastor was saying. She was standing in the middle of the circle Jarrod and I made and when we were done, she looked at me and yelled *"Mommy I feel God!!! WOOOW!!"* We had many moments like that, where she'd have an encounter with the Holy Spirit, so we knew having her do the opening prayer would be perfect.

Our wedding day was awesome. The Salt Covenant the Pastor executed was mind-blowing. He gave us both small black felt drawstring bags with salt in them. He held up a glass box, told us to pour our salt in the box then take turns shaking the box to mix the salt together. The Pastor then opened the box and asked us to use our fingers to take out the salt we put in from our bag and fill our bag back up. It was impossible to do. He told us that's how it should be when either of us try to leave the marriage. We can only divorce if we can take out the salt we put in. It didn't matter who put in how much or when, once it was joined as one, it's one forever.

Everyone was in awe! Little did we know how many trips we'd take to that salt box during our marriage. We both got mad enough to want to break it at times, but we were too afraid to follow through. Felt like Jesus was standing there with His arms folded looking at me with His eyebrow raised daring me to touch it and witness the wrath that will happen. I was to afraid to test Him. God is love, I also knew He was law, so crossing Him or anything He put together disrespectfully would not end well for me.

Anyone who tells you marriage is blissful and romantic and amazing all the time is lying. Two imperfect people trying to represent a perfect covenant is like trying to fly to the moon in a paper airplane. It's the hardest thing you'll ever do. Some years will be amazing, some will have you questioning the quality of your life decisions. Especially marriages ordained by God. The devil hates marriage; it represents power, favor and grace, glorifying God while advancing the Kingdom of Heaven. Marriage is the highest interpersonal relationship one can ever have. Its sacred. That's why it stays under attack. Anything the enemy can do to steal, kill and destroy it, he will try. We knew that going in but living it was different. We saw from our parents the hell that can happen in marriages. The flesh is weak and selfish. It wants what it wants regardless of who it hurts, this intensifies when a Godly marriage is at stake. The bible says in 2 Corinthians 11:14 that *Satan himself masquerades as an angel of light.* That's why it's important to have a strong prayer life and support from other married couples. You will need the spirit of discernment when dating to know the difference between a common flaw that you need to grow through and a red flag you need to stay away from. Many people connect with someone thinking it's a kindred spirit when it's really a common demon or familiar spirit from the enemy disguised as a God sent one. One leads to a messy entanglement the other a heaven-sent engagement!

The food was incredible, everyone was shocked that I did it all myself. We laughed, cried, sang and danced, it was such a great time, but light weight compared to the heavy night we had as Husband and Wife once everyone left! We wasted no time trying to get pregnant with a son and our Big Girl Princess followed up daily asking if he was in my tummy yet, we even let her pick out his name, she chose Aiden, which means *little fire*.

Chapter 2

MYOMECTOMY AND MINISTRY

There's nothing my Husband wanted more than a son. Building a life with him, and raising our daughter changed my heart. I wanted our family to have my DNA in it now too. This should be easy; I didn't have children out of wedlock, I'm married and I'm pro-life! Surely God had no reason to deny me a son, I thought. Women get pregnant every day, many who don't even want their babies, I want mine and will love him endlessly. At the time I didn't know anything about ovulation. I honestly thought you can have sex and get pregnant any day of the month. Everything I set out to do I excel. I win. I lead. I accomplish. I get stuff done - until now. I couldn't work my way through this. There were no calls or meetings I could do. No planning or strategizing would change it. No negotiating or late-night hours, none of the things I'd normally do to make something happen were going to work.

I don't like staying down long, I had to find a way to pull myself out. Especially since there was opposition. An opponent trying to get in my way or someone telling me I can't do something lights my fire. My doctor gave me the plan which was to have a Myomectomy, the surgical removal of fibroids from the uterus. It allows the uterus to be left in place, and for some women, makes pregnancy more likely than before. There are many less invasive options now, but in 2014 a myomectomy was the preferred fibroid treatment for women who want to become pregnant. After surgery I would have to get back on birth control for a year to allow my uterus to heal. With a clear warning from my doctor, that if I get pregnant prior to it healing my *uterus will explode*. After the year I could stop birth control, get on fertility medicine and ta-daa a baby! Although that plan wasn't ideal, it was simple, so I thought. I couldn't have been more wrong.

I had the myomectomy in October 2014 at Memorial Herman Hospital in Houston. My mom came to support, but she was horrible and funny bless her heart. She panics at the thought of anything happening to me. So, while I'm in the waiting room for surgery prep, she decides to comfort me by talking about her hysterectomy of all things. I yell *Ma'am! You are not helping!* My Husband burst out laughing. It was a mess! If that wasn't wild enough, when they roll me out to go get the meds to put me to sleep, she says *Well baby, you're going down the green mile.* Horrible! The Green Mile is a movie about a group of men on death row waiting to be executed! The hallway they walked down to get to their death was called the green mile. Needless to say, she is not allowed in any medical environment with me!

The last thing I remember before surgery was getting the medication to put me to sleep. Surgery was smooth, recovery was horrible. I woke up feeling like I'd been slashed up by the horror characters Jason and Freddy Kruger. It escalated when they were transferring me to the bed in my hospital room. It was four people in the room. They told my husband to step out. One of the nurses on the other side of the bed receiving me was about 4 feet 11 inches tall and really slim. I knew he wasn't going to be strong enough to hold me up. I was a multi-sport varsity athlete and cheerleader in high school; 150 pounds of muscle back then, which was covered with an extra 40 pounds of grown woman weight. I bench press 140 pounds, and the guy they had receiving me on the other side would have been my warm up set! I didn't have my Husband in there to help me communicate. I was telling them to wait and find another nurse to switch out with the small guy because I didn't want him to drop me. They ignored me, and as they lifted me up to transfer me, boom! They dropped me hard on the bed from at least three feet, fresh from major surgery. It was excruciating. I scream. My Husband runs in the room, I tell him they dropped me and then we both gave them a piece of our minds and kicked them all out. It was horrible.

It was the most pain I'd ever experienced in my life. I was about to pass out afterwards on my way to the restroom. Finally, I get home and simple things like pooping or coughing felt like someone was taking a knife to my organs. Walking was hard, sitting straight up, standing up after sitting all were painful. Thankfully my mom was there giving me the nurturing I desperately needed. I'm her only child so this gave her an opportunity to baby me again and I soaked up every bit of it. Thank God for mothers.

December 2014, I'm sitting in the living room with my sister-in-law and Husband talking about the surgery, and how God does things that we don't like sometimes to get us in alignment with what He wants us to do. These are normal talks in our home. Suddenly I hear the Holy Spirit say

My daughters are hungry.

I'm thinking, *Lord why?* Although that's all He said, I knew what He meant. He wanted me to take His word to them as food. My response to Him was filled with childlike defiance.

> *I'm recovering. I don't want to feed anyone. Matter of fact, you fed everyone with the two fish and five loaves, I need somebody to come feed me!*

Then I realized who I was talking to and shut up, just like little kids do when getting out of hand with their parents. He did, after all, make sure the fibroids weren't cancerous, kept me alive during surgery and gave my doctor the skills to keep my uterus intact versus having to get a hysterectomy. That night was the birth of my ministry Straight Talk Woman Talk. I started feeding His daughters January 2015 through a weekly conference call on Mondays. There were hundreds of women who'd get on and thousands more exposed to it weekly. That led up to our first live event, the Straight Talk Woman Talk Intensive in Houston, Tx January 2016. There was so much deliverance, healing and breakthroughs. We continued to build with smaller events called Impart Sessions and The-Equipment across Texas and Georgia and became Straight Talk Woman Talk International with our first event in South Africa January 2018.

Everything is grounded in authenticity and truth with raw unfiltered testimonies with no judgement. Women were honest about their relationship journey with Christ. From loving Him to breaking up with Him and wanting to be an atheist. Sharing their past transgressions of stripping, prostitution, affairs with Pastors, sex with other women, orgies with celebrities, STD's, having countless abortions, physically abusing their husbands, addiction to pornography, drug abuse, the list goes on. Then they'd share how their perspective of who they are in Christ changed and inspired them to rededicate their life to Him. The raw stuff you don't get at a regular Sunday church service. Deliverance was at an all-time high. Immediate healing from sickness and disease would happen for those in attendance. It was truly life changing. No bible college. No super mentor. No ordainment. No religion - all relationship. It was just me, my Bible and Jesus.

That is so important to understand. Many times we allow what others think we should or should not do in ministry dictate our direction. There are so many Pastors and the like who are tremendously insecure and manipulative. I've had friends share with me that when they told their Pastor God told them to do something, the Pastor would respond with *God didn't tell me that about you,* as if you don't have a direct line of communication with Him yourself. Reactions like that are rooted in the spirit of fear and manipulation. Its demonic and unfortunately works on way too many people, leaving you paralyzed, confused and unable to produce. They stay in unhealthy churches for fear of the backlash.

When my husband and I left our last church we were told we were prostituting the church because we'd post a quote from the Pastor on social media and not cite him as the author. What they didn't understand is, that's how we attracted people to join the church. We recruited for membership like we did for our business. The teaching was amazing and we got immediate results from applying it to our life, so we told everyone. People would message us sharing how our post changed their life, we'd reply to them letting them know where we got it from and to come with us to Sunday service or bible study. Yet, because we couldn't be controlled or operate the way they wanted us to, we became the enemy versus them recognizing the real enemy at work. I hope this serves as confirmation for you to be obedient, disconnect from the dysfunction and take the leap. Your obedience to God is worth the temporary sacrifice of a hurt feeling or bruised ego, their approval doesn't lead to your salvation.

The bible says in **Mark 16:20 that He confirms His word with signs following**. The Straight Talk Woman Talk Intensive in South Africa was such a tremendous faith walk. My husband and I were there for business for the third time in October 2017. While visiting the church of our business partner and friend Pinky, God told me again His daughters were hungry. Once again, I was taken back. I thought, *in Africa Jesus? Really? You want me, from Houston, Texas by way of Hearne, Texas to come all the way back to the Continent of Africa down to South Africa to minister to your daughters? You mean no one else who lives here is available?* I was sitting in church rocking back forth while going back and forth with Jesus about this. We just invested tons of money to get there so we could grow our business, and now He's telling me we have to come back in 90 days! I told Him I don't have a problem with it, but this Husband He gave me is different. He's going to have to tell him. I waited for dinner that night to tell my Husband the Lord told me His daughters were hungry in South Africa. To my surprise and dismay, he was excited and supportive. He was supposed to be my out! Now I have to do what the Lord told me to do. We flew back home and I prepared.

God told me to call my friend Arin to reconnect and update on all that's been taking place and that He wanted her to serve alongside me. I knew she was in another country, but I didn't know where. Last I remembered she was in Asia. Her husband works for the U.S. Government so they were living overseas since 2015. They moved before the first Straight Talk Woman Talk Intensive in Houston so she didn't get to experience it, but knew all about it. When I told her what God said about her serving alongside me in South Africa, I asked her where she lived. She tells me they relocated to Botswana, which was only 3 hours away from Johannesburg! She was literally up the road from where the event was going to be! Reluctantly, she agreed to do it. Not because she didn't want to support, but because she thought her support was going to be more for me personally, not necessarily ministering to everyone as well. Little did she and I both know just how much God would use her. We had so much in common with infertility. Her journey was much more complicated on the health side. She had level four endometriosis and fibroids. She'd been doing IVF and IUI with no results. She also was prophesied to that she will have children, yet a decade later, nothing.

   I planned the Straight Talk Woman Talk Intensive on straight faith. I had no budget for it and minimal connections, and God did the miraculous. Over 100 women showed up for a powerful move of God. Miracles were everywhere in that banquet hall! One moment really impacted us. While in prayer Arin laid hands on a woman named Promise to pray for her. We didn't know her personally because everyone who was there I just met during business the trip prior. Promise told us at the event that once Arin prayed for her, she went to the restroom and was bleeding. That's all we knew. After we got back home, she messaged me on Facebook to tell me that she was healed. We learned that she had a miscarriage from fibroids and they didn't get all of the miscarriage out. The event was Saturday and she was scheduled to have surgery on the Tuesday after. She told me in her message *mommy I'm healed* the doctors didn't need to do the surgery because when they did the ultrasound, nothing was there for them to work on.

   Obedience is better than sacrifice. Arin was barren and bleeding herself, but still serving and seeing God's word work through her for someone else. To think, I had the nerves to be upset He wanted me to come back to Africa so quickly. While I worried about the how, I'm thankful I was able to still recognize the Who that handles the how.

God doesn't always do things based on our convenience. His focus is on His covenant. His purpose is for things to be on earth as it is in Heaven and accommodating our flesh isn't a part of that plan. Will He give us peace? Absolutely, but we must participate in His process. Our obedience is critical and worth the sacrifice. If you find yourself constantly stressed, depressed, restless or always a victim, chances are it's not your situation or other people that caused it, it's your disobedience. The stress and heaviness that comes with ignoring an instruction from God is unmatched. The issues at your job, in your relationship, business or illness, in many cases are the fruit of the disobedience root.

- Did you hear a whisper or get a feeling to call someone you don't like or haven't talked to in a while?
- Did you allow the discomfort you felt about it cause you to excuse away the assignment?
- Weeks later do you keep hearing a whisper to do it?
- Do you feel convicted reading this?
- Can't seem to shake it or forget about it and confused as to why?

Red flag alert! Go do it now before you find yourself on the brink of a mental breakdown. I remember when God gave me a Prophetic word for a witch. I didn't want to do it, but I couldn't stop thinking about it. I asked God why would He want someone, especially me, to prophesy to a witch. He knows I don't fool with witches like that! His response was so like Him, *she's still my daughter and I love her.* Then He reminded me of **1 Samuel 16:7,**

> *"Do not look at his appearance or at the height of his stature, because I have rejected him. For the Lord sees not as man sees; for man looks at the outward appearance, but the Lord looks at the heart."*

While I saw her as a witch, He saw her heart. He wouldn't let me rest well until I told her what He said, which ended up not even being about her directly. I felt so much peace after I spoke with her that I cried. It was tears of joy for myself. I was celebrating my growth and how I didn't allow the discomfort to stop me. The best part was that she received the message very well. I'm glad I obeyed! I dare not set myself up to be in the path of God's wrath and you shouldn't either. You're asking God to do the impossible for you with your pregnancy. You may not think that those unrelated things matter, but I assure you they do. God looks at the whole heart, the whole picture. You don't get to pick and choose the areas you want to be Christ-like in. 99% obedience is still 100% disobedience. Repent.

> *Lord, search my heart. Show me where I've fallen short so I can correct it. Your word says in 1 John 1:9, if we confess our sins, you are faithful and just to forgive us our sins and to cleanse us from all unrighteousness. Father, please forgive me. Whatever I need to do to clean up my mess I will do.*

Chapter 3

CLOMID AND FIBROIDS

I continued on with life, ministry and business as usual while we continued to navigate the conception journey. After my doctor confirmed my uterus was healed, I got off birth control and got on a fertility medication called Clomid to help with ovulation. It has an 80% success rate, yet I was part of the 20% it didn't work for. I did 3 rounds of it, it was a horrible experience and felt very manufactured. The prescription came with a calendar of when to take the pills and when to have sex. Romance is extremely important to me. I have to have it. My love language is words of affirmation and physical touch; poems, flowers, cards, hugs, kisses and words in my ear that lift me up and fuel me are what move me. None of which was happening regularly in our marriage at that time, drastically different from how things were when we started dating. My mind and body weren't syncing. My Husband could feel my energy. I remember him telling me that I felt emotionally dead to him. He was right. When we would make love, it wasn't as fun like it was before. In the midst of all of this, I'm still praying over wombs of women, celebrating those who conceived, watching them give birth and thanking me for my love and support, all while barren and broken myself.

After the third round of Clomid I had another ultrasound done for a checkup and my worst nightmare happened. My doctor tells me the fibroids returned and I have two the size of a lemon. At this point I'm drained; I get inside my truck in the parking garage of the hospital, lock the door and scream as loud as I could while crying like a baby. It felt like someone died. I don't remember if I told my husband when I was sitting in the parking garage or when I got home, it's all a blur, I just know that day, April 27, 2017 was a horrible day. I told God and my Husband I'm completely done with medicine and doctors. If we're going to have a son God will just have to just do it because I have nothing left to give and I'm done fighting. I stayed off birth control and just went on with my life. It would be another two years before I went to the doctor again.

In 2018 my nephew and God-Son Zaiden was born. My brother-in-law Kelechi had primary custody. Zaiden's mother wasn't around and I couldn't dare let him go without the warmth of a motherly heart, so I loved and took care of him as if I birthed him myself, just like I did with our daughter. God used him to fill such a large hole in my heart and bring warmth into our home for us all. He is forever MiMi's Z-Baby love!

That season wasn't always great for my marriage though, it was mostly horrible. There were many tough moments. My Husband was upset he didn't have his son, wondering if I'd ever be able to have one. He was prophesied to about his son being the love of his life decades sooner. I was the first woman he ever wanted to have as his wife and mother of his children, and here I am infertile, depressed and uninterested in sex. Not because I wasn't attracted to him, but because I couldn't handle another let down, another missed ovulation, another negative pregnancy test, or another bad report from anyone about anything. Women were created to pro-create; we get pregnant, we carry the seed and we deliver it. I couldn't naturally do what I was made to do as a woman.

Every month my cycle came I'd shed a tear. I'd tell my husband it came and he'd say in a sarcastic tone *good for you.* Felt like a knife in my heart every time. He knew he wanted a son, and with each period it meant no son, so why would he say it was good for me? I felt isolated, attacked and alone. I wanted to react verbally but the Holy Spirit wouldn't let me. I asked God why was my Husband like that and He told me; *he's not being mean, he's sad too, he just doesn't know how to express it.* What I needed was a hug, encouragement and some words filled with love and hope. I was surrounded by people, but felt abandoned. If a woman came on television talking about fertility I'd break down. Someone cuddling their baby on a show, I'd get a lump in my throat. A little boy playing with his father, I'm crying. God forbid something happen to a baby in the news, I'd be a complete mess. Mother's Day was always bitter sweet. We had to celebrate it prior to or after the actual day. Some years I'd get recognized for taking care of our daughter, some I wouldn't, it all depended on what we were arguing about at the time. It was always a gray area, never straight forward like Father's Day where my Husband knew he'd be appreciated. Mother's Day was a reminder that we didn't have our son. I was so tired of doing the unacknowledged and unappreciated work to raise a child I didn't have to agree to raise.

I began to resent my Husband greatly. I'd cry preparing for Father's Day because I wouldn't get a fraction of the effort put in for me on Mother's Day. I wanted to disconnect from our daughter so badly, but the Holy Spirit wouldn't let me, neither would my heart. None of this was her fault. Children don't ask to be born out of wedlock and into dysfunction. She was caught in the middle, she wanted to love me freely, but was constantly being told not to. She asked me one day *Mommy, how do you love someone without hurting someone else for loving the other person?* I told her she shouldn't have to worry about that. I knew what she was talking about and why so I told her that *If I'm the other person you're talking about I want you to know you don't have to do anything for me to know you love me, because regardless I love you with all my heart and there's nothing anyone can do to change that.* She gave me a kiss and laid her head in my lap with her arms wrapped around my waist until she fell asleep as I prayed for her. We had many moments like that. Where she would share her issues or robotically repeat something disturbing, she was told to memorize and say to me. Before I could respond, God would simply whisper *you are what she needs* so I'd sweep my feelings to the side and be in the moment for her.

One day I was in my bedroom folding laundry and she came in to confide in me about something she was told to say to me that she didn't want to say. She was six years old at the time. As I held her in my arms, she asked me to pray for her. Once I was done, she went upstairs to her room to play. About 30 minutes later I hear her coming back downstairs. She walked in my bedroom and said *Mommy I have a surprise for you!* then she handed me a piece of paper she'd cut in half and said with full excitement *It's a card!* When I turned it over, it was a hand drawn flower with the words MOMMY OF GOD written under it. I gave her a big hug and kiss and thanked her for being so sweet and recognizing God in me and I promised her everything will be Ok. Then I reassured her how much I love her. She left out of my room relieved and back to her normal happy self. I cried like a baby. Her writing those words MOMMY OF GOD was complete confirmation from God that I am doing what He called me to do in her life. My example glorified Him so much, that she saw Him in me. No matter how much opposition I faced, nothing was going to change in how I treated her. People would see the love I'd give her and ask us all the time, *when are y'all having a baby? What's the hold up?* I understand it's common to hurry up and get someone to the next level, but what many don't understand is the emotional pressure that causes. Dating couples are constantly asked when will they get married. Graduates are constantly asked when will they get the next degree or start their career. Babies are constantly pushed to be independent. Singles are constantly pressured to settle down. It seems as if no one pauses to think that perhaps their assignment is still active and they will move to the next when led by God, so they can be in alignment with His timing.

When they would ask us, I'd say we're waiting on Jesus; my Husband at times would say he's waiting on me. I'd get so embarrassed and hurt, but would fake laugh like he was kidding and I was Ok. Not only did I not have control over fibroids I also didn't have control over the feelings that came with them. His expectation was for me to just jump on him to have sex all day. Mine was to be prayed for, embraced and pursued so I could have the courage to try again. Typical men are from Mars women are from Venus type stuff. You hear the phrases they've been happily married and in love for twenty-five years. That's romance novel talk. The truth is, they were only happy for about twelve of the twenty-five, and those years weren't consecutive. Love flows in and out, you always care though, I found it better to like. If you don't genuinely like your spouse as a person outside of the marriage, money, sex, business, ministry or whatever you've created together, then you're going to catch hell the times you fall out of love. Jarrod and I were best friends before marriage. It's been that friendship that has kept us linked to love enough to stay married. Even if we did decide to divorce, we'd still be great friends, that's how authentic it is.

We were tested so much I wanted to leave. Although I felt I wanted a divorce many times, I'd never say it because of the power of words. My Husband on the other hand, in all of his Nigerian vigor would actually yell it. He's told me he's wanted a divorce about five times during the first few years of marriage.

I'd tell him Ok. One day I called him to the carpet on it and told him to go get the papers. He snapped back and said they were already ready. I packed my bags and loaded up my 2006 Toyota Scion TC. He changed his tune and asked me where I was going. I told him as far away from him as possible! I didn't go anywhere and he didn't have any divorce papers drawn up, but if he ever served me any during that time, I wouldn't have hesitated to sign them! He knows I'm not like any woman he's been with before; I'm cut from a very different cloth, I may be a Wilkins now but Mitchell runs through my veins and I am without a doubt my father's daughter. I have mastered the gift of goodbye. My never-been-through-a-divorce-before mentality was, I can flip the disconnect switch on regardless of the pain. I felt it would be a very effortless, stress-free break-up. No court necessary and he'd never see me again! We'd been in a relationship since 2010. I rearranged my whole life to care for his child, stood by him during family court battles, got taunted by his ex girlfriends, had to be nice to his wanna be side chicks and constantly go to war in the spirit to salvage our business. I didn't have the desire to fight like that for something with someone who didn't want to be with me.

    I had my whole post-divorce life planned out including lots of newly single sin. I would do all the things I never did and couldn't do professionally because I chose to be in business and a blended family with him. His life required so much of me, and while he never got in the way of what I wanted to do; he was always supportive, it's just that what he needed from me was so time and mentally consuming I couldn't think clear enough, long enough to do what I needed for myself. Thoughts of being single and having my place and life to myself were constant. I'd be in the best shape of my life; dating tall men, at least 6'4' with big feet, big hands, romantic, poetic and having plenty of sex with him without marriage. He'd have an establish career he loved. I wouldn't care if he was an entrepreneur or not, he just couldn't be lazy. He definitely had to have vision and the drive to execute it. Thoughts of the men of my past would come up all the time. Even the two married men who cheated on their wives with me when I was in my 20's. One was a one-night stand with a married escort (yep - they exist. nope - never paid him.) The other was a super-hot and heavy affair with a security guard. That particular one I ended once Jesus slapped me sideways and flipped me like he did the tables in **Matthew 21:12-13**! He made me fight hard for my deliverance from that! I'd gone way too deep. I was on my living room floor in a fetal position crying out to God while listening to Alabaster Box by Cece Winans. He showed me the hell I was in store for and that I was literally one more night with somebody-else's-husband away from total destruction. One thing I know for sure, lust feels like love until it's time to make a sacrifice!

Despite that encounter years prior, my flesh was still dirty during my thoughts of divorce. I'd travel the world, only paying my bills versus attorney fees and child support. The devil had me blown away with all the fun I could have and peace I'd enjoy with all my time for myself. That's a red flag in itself because there is absolutely nothing peaceful about the devil! These thoughts were so intense, I began to attract it into my life. Men would stare at me more in public; randomly tell me how beautiful and sexy I am in a very sensual way, they'd ask if I was single and they didn't care when I said I was married. One guy was literally an exact print out of what my flesh wanted. He knew I was married from my ring, but walked up to me, looked at my ring then looked at me with sultry eyes and said, *are you happy?*

This was the day after the second time my Husband told me he wanted a divorce. I had a sea of chills run through my body. His height made me want to climb him. His lips and smile made me want to kiss him. The sun on his chocolate muscles made me want them wrapped around my body. It felt like an electric wave running through me, it was so intense. Then I literally heard a snap. Someone dropped their bag of groceries with glass bottles in it! It was like a scene from a Lifetime movie! I jumped and thought to myself, Oh hell no! My response to him was so corny I couldn't do anything else, I yelled with my eyes closed tight and rolling my neck, *boy if you don't get your incubus behind away from me. It doesn't matter if I'm not happy right now, I'm in covenant with the Lord Jesus the Christ and my Husband, goodbye!* I kept my eyes closed tight, turned around and started praying in the spirit on the way to my car.

I never made it in the store and didn't go back for a while. I was having all those lustful thoughts and didn't even know the dude's name! I never saw him before that day and haven't seen him since. He was definitely a demon! It was very flattering, and the opposite of the words I was hearing at home, but even though it felt so so so good to be desired for that moment I knew better. It's just like the enemy to tempt you with only the things your flesh likes. I'd always say something crazy to myself when tempted. *To hell with him! He probably has syphilis, gonorrhea, chlamydia, trichomoniasis and 25 kids by 20 women, and is a part-time prostitute for men!*

He could really be a good guy, but for the sake of my salvation he must be the devil. Then I'd thank God for my Husband, his baggage, my baggage and our baggage together. I know what I have and whether I like it all the time or not, it's mine and God is in it so that's where I will be.

With all of this fleshly activity going on I knew something was brewing in the spirit. My sinful thoughts were way too intense. There was something the enemy wanted to distract me with so he could steal, kill and destroy what God was sending to me. I kept asking God *why is this dramatic journey so necessary? Why can't you just do it? Why did things have to be so intense?*

He'd answer me, but it wouldn't be until much later.

Chapter 4

CLEANING HOUSE

I realized that while I was praying for everyone else, I was complaining about my situation. I wasn't praying for my own marriage and I wasn't praying for myself, not like I knew I could and should. Praying for me required me to change and I don't know of anyone who willingly enjoys signing up for that. Especially when the Holy Spirit is the one leading the change! Things began to intensify at home, it was like I was living in the twilight zone. My marriage was under attack and our daughter was doing some serious rebelling. Nobody looked and acted like the people I'd grown to love. One night I told God, *you have my undivided attention now*. When I woke up the next morning, I realized I was trying to fix a spiritual problem naturally and that will never work. I went on a fast, grabbed my anointing oil and cleansed my home.

I burned and threw out everything that was brought into my house from someone I didn't trust. There was a fish tank brought into our home; it had been there a few weeks, I was praying one day and asked the Holy Spirit to show me what I needed to get rid of. I walked into the kitchen later and the Holy Spirit said *the fish tank*. I know animals are used in witchcraft so I immediately got my anointing oil, laid hands on it while saying over and over *I plead the blood of Jesus* then I started speaking in tongues (a prayer language only God understands). The next day the fish was dead and the water inside was brown. Needless to say, Bubbles didn't get a burial! We just dumped the whole tank in the back yard and carried on. It wasn't his fault his owner had demonic motives, but it was his problem. Nobody and nothing was safe!

    I don't know about you, but I get fired up when God speaks in such a bold, obvious and immediate way like that. I was definitely shaking things up in the spirit realm from doing the work I knew needed to be done. I'd play deliverance prayers on the TV from YouTube throughout the house and when I'd try to rewind it, an orange cartoon looking cat would sit on the circle cursor on the screen and the circle would shake back and forth like a tug of war between me and the cat. It wanting to fast forward the message and end it and me rewinding it. The second time it happened it was a brown dog. There are many levels and layers to the spiritual world. I know people who have traveled deep depths into them. It takes a special kind of person to be able to handle all that comes with that. It's not a game. Most would be afraid to encounter what I had. The me in my twenties definitely would've been. I didn't get my first bible as an adult until twenty-three.

    I remember when some ministers tried to teach me to speak in tongues when I lived in Ohio. I went to church one Sunday and during alter call they had a line for those who wanted to speak in tongues. I got in line, they took me to the back of the church and sat me in a chair in a room with two other women. They said all I had to do was keep saying Jesus over and over and I'd get it *the tongues* as they called it. After about 30 minutes of Jesus-ing and only thinking about what I was going to eat when I left, I told them I'd have to learn some other time. I left and never returned to that church again. I didn't get my prayer language until a couple of years later.

Here I was now in my mid-thirties and matured in Christ to the point where spiritual warfare wasn't a scary thing anymore, it was fuel. The Holy Spirit revealed to me this was a deep clean. I was digging up demonic roots and had many Angels working on my behalf. The devil was making it easy for me to strategize and fight because his attacks were so predictable. I had so much confidence, I could feel the presence of God sitting in the midst of my home covering me. I continued my fast while the prophetic dreams and God-sent prophecies from others came in like a flood.

Chapter 5

PROPHETIC ENCOUNTERS

Supernatural Birthing

In July 2018 I was an emcee for my friend Apostle Andrea Haynes' ministry event. She had her mentor Apostle David Boyd there from Mississippi, along with his daughter and a few other church members. The second day of the event his daughter began to prophesy about fertility. She said *there is one person here who is struggling with getting pregnant. If that is you, come forward.*

I took off my heels and ran to the front of the room with my arms up yelling - *that's me!*

She brought her father to the altar and he shared how his ministry specializes in fertility. He brought with him multiple women who were told they would never conceive, but later did after being connected to their ministry. One woman walked up behind him holding her son. The others came to the altar as Andrea laid hands on my stomach, and he laid hands my head and prayed. My husband was standing by my side with his hand on my back while Apostle Boyd said:

> *"By this time next year, there will be noise in the house. You will give birth and once you do your ministry will take off. Your story will cause a super natural birthing for so many women all over the world."*

I believed every word.

September 2018: Ariana Prophecy

My husband and I were in Florida for business. We'd been practically living there, working through the week meeting with leaders from all over the US, Canada, Australia and Mexico, going home on the weekends to do laundry and make sure the house was good. We were working around the clock.

One night we were meeting in our hotel suite with our friends from Australia who we flew in town, when I get a text message from one of my prophetic sisters Ariana. She and I met in church years before and she'd been on my mind that week. I figured it was because she was into health and nutrition and that is the industry we were doing business in at the time. I planned on calling to her to meet once I got back to Houston, then I get a text from her.

Ariana: *Hey Lady! This is Ariana. Checking to see if this is still your number.*

Me: *Heeeeey!!! Yes it is. I promise I was just thinking of you today!*

Ariana: *I have a Word for you. Can I call really quick?*

Me: *Yes!*

I go to the bedroom and the phone rings. We do a little small talk but she gets right into it.

> *The Lord showed me you in my dream. I see you doing ministry on a big scale. He said you were a mother of Nations. I keep seeing you with a baby. The Lord said, because she has taken care of mine, I will take care of hers. I see you in a higher position with all these daughters around you. Then I saw a tube inserted into your uterus, then the cells formulating and turning blue. In the Heavens your baby is ready to be implanted. Its a boy.*

I immediately get excited. Nothing like a true Prophet sent from God to share a word to activate your faith. I was so happy because my Husband and I had made love the night before! He was just as excited and I was when I told him the news. The next week we flew her in to Florida to meet for business as well. While there our business partners were hosting a women's conference at their church. It was around 5:00p when the receptionist told me about it. I told her I'd try to make it since we had so many people to meet with that night. Ariana had just landed when I told her about the conference and that I wanted her to go with me. She rushed to get dressed and we followed one of our business partners and her daughter to their church. As we're walking up to the church, I felt the ground shake like an earthquake. I stopped to get my balance, then took another step and it happened again. I looked at Ariana and said *did you feel that?!?* She said *My God Yes!* We hadn't even made it into the building yet and the Spirit of the Lord was so heavy. She grew up in California and although she'd been gone many years since moving to Texas, she didn't forget what an earthquake felt like. Needless to say, it was a powerful night and just a preview of what was to come.

January 2019: Stadium of Elizabeth's

By this time my cycle had come and gone on through the new year, and so did my depression. The prophetic word increased my faith, but my flesh still couldn't handle the current reality. I still wasn't pregnant. The prophecy from Ariana hit different because it was so specific. I hadn't had that much anticipation before. I'd even began looking for baby stuff.

Everyone wants to be prophesied to, but most don't understand is there is a process that comes with it. Could it be instant? Yes. But it can also be years down the road. Many forfeit the prophecy because they don't have enough faith to be patient through the process. I was no different, every month I saw blood on my pantyliner from my cycle I'd go through an emotional whirlwind.

One day I was on my way to the beauty supply store in our old neighborhood where my apartment was when I received a text message from another prophetic sister Garlinda. We were in business together, but hadn't spent any time together personally, so she didn't know my story or journey, but she knew God. He put her on my heart a few months prior. I'd asked her to share on my Straight Talk Woman Talk – Activate Your Faith series. She agreed, but later declined. We kept communicating through social media, so when she messaged me one day, I was excited to connect.

Garlinda: *Hi Porshea can you call me when you have the opportunity? It's about something totally unrelated to business, its ministry related.*

Me: Hey lady! I'm free now. Will call ya.

Garlinda: *Thank you so much.*

When she told me that it was ministry related, I figured it had to do with her joining me for Straight Talk Woman Talk. Instead, she had a Word the Lord knew I desperately needed in that exact moment. We have small talk and she shares:

> *The Spirit of the Lord keeps showing me you with a baby. Do you want to have a baby?* I said yes. She says, *ok, well the Lord wanted me to tell you that you will have a baby. That He will do it His way and to relax and trust Him.*

Simple yet powerful and definitely on time because I was emotionally weak. My faith was wavering; I wasn't going to stop believing, but I was so tired. I literally just finished crying in the parking lot in front of the beauty supply store when she messaged me. I'm so glad she was obedient and even more glad I agreed have a call with her.

God sends us His willing vessels. The bible says we know in part and prophecy in part. There's the spirit of prophesy, gift of prophesy and word of knowledge then office of the prophet. All of which you are born into. So, a prophetic word may not always be exact, but when led by God, He will give you just the amount of information you need to know He's working. One-man plants, another waters, and another gets the harvest. Even if you don't understand anything a real Prophet shares, the least you should know is God is moving. I'm so grateful for every right standing prophetic voice He has raised. That's a gift to be honored and respected tremendously.

There was a big conference we were attending for business with over 10,000 people in a stadium. After what I'd experienced in the parking lot on the way to the women's event I was looking forward to the conference, especially since the night before they have a full worship service. We get to the worship night with our associates and they begin to choose different people to share their testimonies.

For behold, when the sound of your greeting reached my ears, the baby in my womb leaped for joy. - Luke 1:44

One after another were stories of women and their infertility testimonies. I was a complete mess. *What does this have to do with business?* I thought. I fought back tears as hard as I could but I had to let them flow. One testimony in particular stayed with me. It was a woman named Rinda who had given birth to a preemie named Presley. Presley was a fighter, and her mommy and daddy were prayer warriors, but after months in the NICU, the Lord called her home. The fact Rinda was able to stand on stage and share that testimony shows the power of God and of His daughters. They'd created a non-profit to continue on the legacy of their Angel baby girl, geared towards helping parents navigate the NICU journey. There's so much care for the child, but there wasn't much for the parents, so they created it in Presley's memory.

I bawled like a baby. Thanking God for my journey and for all the women around me who have fought and overcome battles I couldn't even imagine going through. I was tremendously inspired to believe big again and trust God's timing. I felt so loved by God that He'd use an entire stadium of His daughters just to encourage me. I was full. Every woman who shared was white, which made me think of the cultural differences when it comes to things like this. It reminded me how alone I felt when I got fibroids. Now that I look back, I know it was fertilizer for what He'd call me to do today. I remember in 2014 He showed me in a dream a picture of me walking onto a large stage with bright lights. In the dream I was standing in the back close to the curtains watching myself walk to the center of the stage. The light parts and I see a sea of women in the audience. Thousands of them in a stadium praising God. I believe wholeheartedly there will be stadiums of Supernatural Mamas coming together to activate their faith in-fertility and testify about their supernatural pregnancies.

April 2019: Besties Belief Building Baby

Jenn and I met when I was in high school and she was a freshman in college. We both were working at a retail store in the mall. I was a keyed associate on my path to management and she was a sales associate joining the team to work through the Holiday season. She reported to me and would call me ma'am. I'd let her, even though I knew I was just sixteen. She continued until one day she heard me talk about something in high school, and she asked how old I was. She fussed at me for letting her call me ma'am even though I was younger. I thought it was funny. We were inseparable from then on. Time would pass over the years and we'd go months without talking at times, but would pick up as if no time had gone by. As we got older, we always said we'd have kids at the same time, and travel the world.

Even though we were close I didn't tell her about my fibroids or myomectomy. I didn't want to share anything negative, since she'd had so many miscarriages and was still trying. I remember the day I did eventually share, it was about four months after my surgery. I was in the church parking lot after bible study when she called. She began to talk about her most recent miscarriage, and that it was because of fibroids. She also hadn't heard of them before. They feed off of estrogen, which our body produces a lot of to fuel the baby. The fibroids had over taken the baby so there was no longer a heartbeat on the ultrasound. She was too far long for the doctors to remove the baby, so she had to deliver it.

I cried when she said the nurses were telling her to push, and after a couple of times of them saying it, she finally yelled *I don't know how!* They didn't know that was her first experience with giving birth. For years she'd been my big sister, now it was my time to be hers. The next thing she had to do was the myomectomy. She was afraid and needed a sister, that's why she called me. When I told her I'd just had mine, she was blown away and relieved that she could get preparation from someone she trusted. I gave her the full story; told her what underwear to buy so her cut wouldn't get agitated from her bikinis, what to expect during the first poop afterwards, even what to tell the hospital staff beforehand so she wouldn't get dropped like I did. We cried and laughed and prayed. Her surgery went great and her recovery was smooth, she was back to herself and trying again for a baby in no time. I admire her strength to persevere. All I could think was how I couldn't do what she did and handle it how she had. God knows what battles to give to who.

A couple of years later I was sitting on the couch one night and I get a text message from her in our sister language:

Jenn: *Hiiiiiiiiiiiiiiiii!! Are you in America?*

Me: *(laughing emojis) Hiiiiiiiiiiiii! Yes!!! You totally said that like a valley girl.*

Her: (laughing emojis) You like have to call me right now before I fall asleep.

She always worked out at 5:00a so I was shocked she was up. I immediately called her.

Me: OMG what?!

Jenn: Well, I'm pregnant.

Me: SHUT UP!!!!!!!

I hit the FaceTime button because I had to see her. She answers it, I see her belly and we do our sister scream. I'm jumping up and down like we normally do, she just bounces because she can't get her feet off the ground. It was the cutest bump ever! I'm crying she's crying, it's a faith activating moment for sure. I asked her when did she know she was pregnant and she shares they did In vitro fertilization (IVF). IVF is a method of assisted reproduction in which a man's sperm and a woman's eggs are combined outside of the body in a laboratory dish. One or more fertilized eggs (embryos) may be transferred into the woman's uterus, where they may implant in the uterine lining and develop.

I sit there in shock because I'd been vacillating on whether or not that was the route for me! I always felt God would do it naturally, but because it was taking so long and I had complications I didn't know if I should take a different route. I didn't know anyone personally who did IVF, so I just kept it in the back of my mind versus pursuing it. When she shared her story, I took this as confirmation it was something I should take a serious look into. She shared her experience with it, details on the shots, how much it cost, the doctor visits, everything. She was the big sister again walking me through something I thought I was going to have to go through as well, just like I walked her through the myomectomy. I was now much more open to doing IVF, but I still didn't have complete peace that's what God wanted me to do. I was struggling between how I wanted it to go, because I hate medical procedures, and making sure I wasn't imposing my will for what I wanted over God's. Sometimes we can be stubborn in our faith and belief in something, it blocks our visibility to the full picture God wants us to see. So, since I wasn't clear - I didn't do anything.

May 2019: Petty Peninnah

We all have someone in our life who dislikes or even hates us, whether we know them or not. Nobody likes everybody all the time. Peninnah is woman mentioned briefly in **1 Samuel chapter 1**. She represents a jealous, envious, and divisive spirit. Someone who thrives on your short-comings. They take pride and joy in your setbacks and always see fit to remind you of anything negative from your past. They're never happy for you, because they are unhappy with themselves.

1 Samuel 1:2, 6: *By taking Peninnah as his second wife, Elkanah brought much sorrow to his first godly wife, Hannah. Peninnah has no record apart from the fact that she lived in Ramah, was the wife of Elkanah and the mother of his children. Because of her initial barrenness, Hannah became the target of Peninnah's jealousy, and her life was a constant fret through her rival's tantalizing. If ever there was a heartless woman it was Peninnah. Her provocation became intensified because of Elkanah's love and tenderness toward Hannah whose heart often smarted from Peninnah's jealous thrusts. But Hannah's patience, self-control and intercession prevailed and she became the mother of Samuel who was "more than a prophet"*

I thank God for giving me composure like Hannah. Every year around Mother's Day Peninnah gets extra active for me. She would make comments to me directly or through a third party, about my infertility. Even going as far as telling our daughter that I'll forget all about her when I have a baby. To have this little person come sit in my lap at five years old with tears in her eyes, telling me this was heart breaking. It goes to show how jealously and envy are selfishly blinding. Peninnah was so focused on hurting me and breaking the bond our daughter and I had that she'd break the child's heart to do it.

One day I was taking our daughter to school when she shared with me that Peninnah told her that *Daddy was having a baby.* Poor baby was so was upset because she thought I was pregnant and didn't tell her first. I let her know I wasn't and I don't know why Peninnah would say that. I also told her that when it happens, we'd never tell Peninnah because it's not her business, but she would be the one to tell Peninnah if she chose to. To which our daughter said, *"I'm not going to tell her I have a brother until he's one year old."*

I know Peninnah goes to people she calls healers, which is another term for witch. My Husband shared some of the things she'd try to get him to do when they were together, which contributed greatly to him knowing he didn't want her to be his wife. She has a very jealous spirit and always acts up when something positive happens in our family, she's very predictable, we can countdown to when we'll hear something from her. Usually, its immediate - a crazy email, text message or something to create conflict. I'm never shocked when she begins to stir up, just annoyed like walking through a cloud of gnats. She even made the same comment of *your daddy's having a baby* to my husband the day before. He never told me about it because he literally blocks out everything and anything she says or does. He just acts like she doesn't exist because he wishes she didn't.

We get to the school for Mother's Day breakfast, I always go at the request of our daughter. Peninnah is there and we're standing together with the teacher in the library when she says:

Peninnah: *Did Jarrod tell you what I said?*

Me: *No he never mentions you.*

Peninnah: *Well, I said your daddy is having a baby.*

Me: I laughed and said *Oh wow!*

Peninnah: *I didn't know if I was spilling the beans or not.*

Me: *I don't know! Are youuu??*

We fake laugh and continue on to get books for our daughter, who is standing there looking at us like we're crazy. I'm annoyed because she's doing this in front of the child and the teacher in the middle of the library! We checkout the book and make our way to the school office to wait for some paperwork and she brings it up again. At this point I'm frustrated, not for me but for our daughter. She wanted nothing more than to be a big sister. She named her brother Aiden when we got married in 2014. She talked about him constantly over the years, we all did as if he was already with us. This comment of your daddy's having a baby and constantly bringing it up wasn't hurting me as intended. It was hurting the child.

Peninnah didn't know how much of a bond that subject was for our family. I could see the tears well up in our daughters' eyes, she desperately wanted to be a big sister. When Peninnah brought it up again I changed the subject. I looked at our daughter and said:

Me: I don't know when he's coming, we're gonna just have to put in a call to Jesus!

Our daughter: *We sure are because He's taking forever!*

Then I told her that he's coming and will love her so much especially when she changes all his poopy diapers. She laughs of course and that changes the mood. At that point Peninnah realized she wasn't going to get the reaction out of me she wanted, so she didn't push the conversation further, even though I could see she was eager to do so. It was so random, I couldn't understand why she was doing it. We'd become so great at removing her from our thoughts and life that nothing she ever did registered as the pettiness she intended. We tried to co-parent healthily, but she always kept driving division. By any means she would say whatever she could to our daughter or me to create discord. We had a few run ins in the beginning where I'd respond, then my husband and I both saw there was no way to reason with her, because she was unhappy and that unhappiness wasn't ours to fix nor deal with.

She'd done many things over the years, including going up to my mother's job. My mom worked at a child care center for a bank, they had very strict rules and employees weren't allowed to have visits. She decided to pop up one day, uninvited and unwanted. My mom sent my Husband and I a text concerned that she was there, wondering if she was mentally Ok because she was sitting in the foyer with a blank stare. My mother wasn't close with her at all, and only communicated about pick up or drop off when my Husband and I traveled, so we were all shocked that she was there. I told my mom I doubt she'd do anything, but to notify security to document it on the security cameras and to also be mindful of her surroundings when going to her car, just in case. Going to my mothers job was a direct attack at me. Like I said, Peninnah is a taunting spirit filled with jealousy and envy. Her goal was to get a reaction from me, but what she didn't know is I don't fight fair. My reaction will never be in the natural, I go to war in the spirit, I understand the person isn't the problem, the principality is - that is who I fight. When I drove away from the school, I heard the Holy Spirt say:

"He's close".

I immediately began to praise. Maybe one of her witch friends said something because she's never been that desperate to get information from me. She usually just sticks to stalking on social media which we don't care about, but this was different so he must be really on the way! I was so fired up! I sang all the way home! I called my friend Keisha who's in ministry as well, to tell her what happened. She tells me about Hannah's story in the bible **1 Samuel 1:28** and her being taunted by Peninnah. The Holy Spirit led me to the book of Samuel earlier that week, but I missed that particular part. I knew of Hannah, but hadn't read her story, when I did it blew me away.

The elders would always say there is nothing new under sun. That is so true. Who knew they'd have this kind of drama in the Bible days! Considering everything else that went on during those times, it was refreshing to see. I now had a reference point to hold onto for conquering that demon. Peninnah was only mentioned those seven verses in 1 Samuel. Her journey was short. Remember that the next time you're taunted. Let your belief in God and His promises to you be greater than anyone or anything trying to tell you different. They're just attempting to use you as a scapegoat for their own insecurities and poor decisions.

Jealousy and envy are bitter roots that run deep. Should the Peninnah's of the world take a serious moment to reflect on their journey of life from childhood, they'll understand their unhappiness started long before you entered their life. Pray for them. That's what I did. Yes, I brought Holy Ghost fire down in warfare, but I also prayed for God to restore her heart. I didn't want to, but God told me to do it so I did. He told you to pray for your enemies as well.

> Matthew 5:44 - But I say to you, love [that is, unselfishly seek the best or higher good for] your enemies and pray for those who persecute you.

The next night I have a prophetic dream so powerful it shifted everything for me in activating my faith.

Chapter 6

TIME TO POST UP

Post up is a term black people used when we'd gather somewhere, usually in the club or convenience store parking lot. It was also used when you had beef with someone. You'd post up on your block and if the enemy came through they'd either keep driving by because they saw you were ready for whatever or they'd stop and you'd show them you were ready for whatever and fight. My posting up growing up was hanging out with friends in the parking lot after a party or something. The fellas called it parking lot pimping. They'd use that time to try and get phone numbers of the girls in the club.

Spiritual warfare is the same. We hold no punches with the enemy. When we post up we're giving notice that we're ready for war. PeriodT!

May 7, 2019 - Ocean Dream

    I was at the beach with my Husband and our extended family. All the Nigerians and Americans were laughing, dancing and eating, like we were at a family reunion or something.

My God-Son Zaiden was hanging out with me, then he ran off to play. A few moments go by and I don't see him anywhere. I looked around the tent and no Zaiden. I begin to panic, but everyone else kept on like nothing was wrong. I look towards the shore and I see 3 drag marks in the sand from the restaurant to the ocean. I hear the Holy Spirit say:

He's in the water.

It's night time and there was no way to see anything in the water, but I was going to jump in anyway. When I ran towards the shore to jump in the Holy Spirit said:

Don't get in, pray.

I stopped at the first drag mark and stretched my arms to pray hard. There were two people with me praying, one on my left and one on my right. I don't know who they were I just felt their presence. When I stretched my arms to pray at the first drag mark the water receded back some and when it came back to shore Zai's toy washed up, making me feel like there was more there. The Holy Spirit said:

Keep going.

By this time the family notices what's going on and starts panicking, but no one came to the ocean where I was. I ran to the second drag mark, stretched my arms to pray and the water receded back further. When it came back to shore his back pack I bought him for school washed up. I yelled to the two people with me *he's close!!*

I ran to the third drag mark, stretched my arms out to pray, the water receded so far back this time you could see the ocean floor for miles, like it would do in a tsunami. This time when the water came back to shore my nephew came with it sitting on top of what looked like a medical device or robot holding an empty bottle of alcohol laughing as if nothing happened.

I woke up terrified with tears running down my face, my pillow was soaking wet from the tears and sweat. I looked at the clock on my phone and it was 3:33am. 3 is my Kingdom number and how God communicates to me, 3:33am is also the time I was born.

> *Jeremiah 33:3 'Call to Me and I will answer you, and tell you [and even show you] great and mighty things, [things which have been confined and hidden], which you do not know and understand and cannot distinguish.'*

Jeremiah was born a Prophet, but struggled with believing he could do what God called him to do because of his young age. Jeremiah didn't go to bible college, neither did I, but bible college wasn't a requirement for our calling. It didn't even exist in his day, neither was a spiritual rank appointment by another spiritual leader.

> *Jeremiah 1:5 "Before I formed you in the womb I knew you [and approved of you as My chosen instrument], and before you were born I consecrated you [to Myself as My own]; I have appointed you as a prophet to the nations." 6 Then I said, "Ah, Lord God! Behold, I do not know how to speak, For I am [only] a young man." 7 But the Lord said to me, "Do not say, 'I am [only] a young man,' Because everywhere I send you, you shall go, And whatever I command you, you shall speak. 8 "Do not be afraid of them [or their hostile faces], For I am with you [always] to protect you and deliver you," says the Lord. 9 Then the Lord stretched out His hand and touched my mouth, and the Lord said to me, "Behold (hear Me), I have put My words in your mouth. 10 "See, I have appointed you this day over the nations and over the kingdoms, to uproot and break down, to destroy and to overthrow, to build and to plant."*

Like Jeremiah, I was born a Prophet. It just took the first 3 decades of my life for me to get close enough to God to know it. He decided who we were before He formed us in our mother's womb. We were already who He created us to be in Spirit. Our spiritual life in Heaven preceded our natural life. Heaven is our home country, and God, Elohim, Yahweh, our Father is the King. The Bible (Old and New Testament) is our guideline and bill of rights as legal citizens of the Kingdom of Heaven and children of the King of all kings. That's where our true identity is, but because of the fall of man (Adam – **Genesis**) we as humans aren't born knowing it, but instead are born into discovering it. We have to fight through the limiting beliefs of the world and the words of hurt people hurting people. Family, friends, TV, social media are all focused more on telling us who we should be in a career versus teaching us how to understand the Word of God, so we know who we are supposed to be in our calling. Its hard for someone to teach us who we are called to be when they didn't create the call nor have gone through the experience with Christ to learn and understand their own.

Back to the ocean dream. My Husband was sleeping next to me, so I quietly got out the bed to sit on the floor and pray for my nephew. I wrote the dream down then sent a voice note the next day to my friend Dr. Alexis. We met years earlier at a ministry event. We both were speakers and connected afterwards. She is a Prophet as well, so I asked her what she thought it meant. The medical device and empty bottle of alcohol really had me lost especially since I don't drink. I also told her about my Peninnah encounter. A couple of days later Alexis replies via text:

Alexis: Your dream
3:33 is your promise concerning your child
Zaiden – represent your son
Ocean – represents marine kingdom
He was seated on a robot meaning technology, I think the Lord is saying its ok to seek technology concerning pregnancy and to be sober about your decision. Be sober and vigilant cause the enemy roams around like a lion looking for whom he will devour (paraphrased).

Me: 3:33 is also the time I was born. My mom told me that years after God revealed the number to me. She said she forgot.
Marine Kingdom – wow. Didn't even know that existed! Definitely reading up on it. No fear. Especially now that I have more knowledge. Its ignorance the enemy uses against us.
Wow – regarding robot and technology. Alcohol and being sober about decision. That is great revelation because it is an area of hesitation for me. Not being patient – Ishmael.

In the Bible (**Genesis 16**) Sara was impatient with her infertility and so desperate for Abraham to have a baby that she gave him permission to have one with the maid Hagar. Hagar gave birth to Ishmael. All was fine until (**Genesis 21**) after Sarah got pregnant with her promise baby Isaac and sent Hagar and Ishmael off to the desert because Hagar was mocking Isaac. This caused a lot of turmoil because Abraham loved his son. This would've been a hot episode for Jerry Springer or Maury! For me, the lesson was to not be so desperate for a child that I do the wrong thing and create an unnecessary problem for myself. I knew IVF was an option but I never felt in my heart that it was what God wanted me to do. I was never at peace with it, but I also wanted to make sure I wasn't using my faith to be stubborn. So, I did nothing with it.

The Holy Spirit gave me a list of women to contact and share this dream with. It activated their faith greatly as many of them desired to conceive as well.

Chapter 7

FAITH ACTIVATION

July 2019

Things began to intensify. Opposition. More dreams. More prophesies. Random people at random places:

"Hey Porshea do you want a son?"

Me: *Yes.*

Them: *Ok the Lord said you will have one.*

A few months prior Dr. Alexis shared a video on social media of another Prophet named Tiphani. My baby leaped listening to her so I began to follow her and saw she was hosting an event in Washington, DC the weekend of the fourth of July called Millions Conference. I immediately booked my travel, it was my first non-business overnight trip alone in years. Things were crazy at home, so I was ready to get away. I went expecting a Word from the Lord and I got so much more.

It was over 3,000 people there from multiple countries. The content was a perfect blend of Kingdom and business. Tiphani began to minister and pray about fibroids. Soon as she did I felt a wind. She said they were an attack from the enemy. This was the first time I'd ever heard anyone minister about fibroids and it wasn't until that moment that I realized I was dealing with them all wrong. I didn't see them as an attack from the enemy, but it made sense after hearing that because no one can explain why 80% of black women have them. The Holy Spirit said to me

It's because of who you're giving birth to.

We teach what we know, but can only reproduce who we are and when you know who you are in Christ, you have a greater understanding of who you will give birth to. My son will go on to do greater things than my husband and I. The enemy doesn't want another prophet, pastor, evangelist, etc.... in the world so if he can stop the conception or get in a pregnant woman's head enough to convince her to have an abortion, then he wins.

In that moment at millions I saw everything differently. Shortly after Tiphani spoke another Prophet took the stage named Sophia. The Lord delivered her from homosexuality and completely transformed her life. Her spirit is so warm and welcoming, then she begins to prophesy and out comes major Holy Ghost fire! I remember standing in the back of the room with my back up against the wall and no one behind me. She told us to pray in the Spirit for what we were believing God for, then she said:

When I count to three, you're going to be pushed into your next level!

The moment she yelled *3!* I felt a massive hand in the middle of back pushing me forward so hard I had to run to the corner to vomit. When I gathered myself I heard the Lord say loudly

> *Get back on your post!*

I left that event feeling 1,000 feet tall and demon proof. Being in the presence of other Prophets sharpened and fueled me. I went back home and posted up ready for whatever. I multiplied my warfare. God had told us it was time to move so we chose a larger house that had two bedrooms downstairs to accommodate my mother who had knee issues. This new house stirred Peninnah up who was manipulating our daughter and causing her to act out. My Husband had a health scare. Then, in the midst of packing and cleaning I found more things to burn and destroy. I couldn't wait to get out that house! I called Apostle Andrea to tell her all that's been going on. I realized I hadn't told her about the Ocean Dream and my wavering with IVF. When I do, she yells:

> *PORSHEA!! You got your baby!! You called him forth yourself out of the enemy's hand!*

I hadn't thought about it that way. She was right. He was with me now; my faith was so stirred up. She tells me Apostle Boyd's daughter called her a couple of weeks prior to tell her she had a dream that I was pregnant and had shown her an ultra-sound picture. That fired me up even more! Especially since it was a year after her father prophesied to me about getting pregnant. All could remember was him saying *by this time next year there will be noise in the house.*

I thought the noise was going to be a crying baby, instead it was me posting up and going to war! Then it hit me. I'd been going to war so hard in the heavens the enemy took advantage of my ignorance of the marine kingdom and hid my son there so I began to pray against spirits there too. God knew all of this so He took me to the ocean in my dream to get my son, using my love for Zaiden as the draw. That's why the Holy Spirit told me not to get in the water but instead to pray at it. Complete revelation!

My Son Aiden was now with me! My faith was activated!

Spiritual warfare isn't a game, nor something to take lightly otherwise you begin attract things into your life that weren't even intended for you. You have to be armored up, with the full armor of God as in **Ephesians 6:10-18**

The Armor of God

"In conclusion, be strong in the Lord [draw your strength from Him and be empowered through your union with Him] and in the power of His [boundless] might. Put on the full armor of God [for His precepts are like the splendid armor of a heavily-armed soldier], so that you may be able to [successfully] stand up against all the schemes and the strategies and the deceits of the devil. For our struggle is not against flesh and blood [contending only with physical opponents], but against the rulers, against the powers, against the world forces of this [present] darkness, against the spiritual forces of wickedness in the heavenly (supernatural) places. Therefore, put on the complete armor of God, so that you will be able to [successfully] resist and stand your ground in the evil day [of danger], and having done everything [that the crisis demands], to stand firm [in your place, fully prepared, immovable, victorious]. So, stand firm and hold your ground, having tightened the wide band of truth (personal integrity, moral courage) around your waist and having put on the breastplate of righteousness (an upright heart), and having strapped on your feet the gospel of peace in preparation [to face the enemy with firm-footed stability and the readiness produced by the good news]. Above all, lift up the [protective] shield of faith with which you can extinguish all the flaming arrows of the evil one. And take the helmet of salvation, and the sword of the Spirit, which is the Word of God."

With all prayer and petition pray [with specific requests] at all times [on every occasion and in every season] in the Spirit, and with this in view, stay alert with all perseverance and petition [interceding in prayer] for all God's people."

The next day I called my doctor to make an appointment for a pap smear and full exam. I hadn't been since the fibroids came back in 2017, so I knew I needed a check up on them before attempting anything with IVF. I'd been working out with a trainer, eating clean and lost thirty pounds, my body would be in a much better position now to carry. A few days after I made my doctor's appointment, they called me to cancel it. I was so upset. All the fighting it took to get to the point where I'd decide to go back to the doctor and they cancel on me? Angry was an understatement. They asked me if I wanted to pick another date, I told them no and hung up the phone.

August 2019

Dr. Alexis did her normal monthly word and that month it was Govern: to exercise continuous sovereign authority over; to control and direct the making of. This was a word for me. Confirming my authority in my home. I govern, rule, control, direct what happens there not the enemy or anyone outside of my family. That means I go to war and what I say goes. Every authority must yield to mine. I have the blue print. I have my son, now it's just a matter of staying in alignment with God's time. I began to commit the first hour of every morning to praying over my womb and for my son.

I'd play and sing You Are Great my Juanita Bynum then go into prayer.

For you deserve the glory, and the honor.
I lift my hands in worship and I bless your Holy name.
You deserve the glory, all the honor.
I lift my hands in worship and I bless your Holy name.
Cause you are great.
You do miracles so great.
There is no one else like you.
No one else like you.

Father I thank you and I honor you. You are great and greatly to be praised, there is none like you. I plead the blood of Jesus over myself, from the crown of my head to the souls of my feet. I pray that you keep me from evil, hurt, harm, danger, death and destruction. I plead the blood of Jesus over my womb. I cancel fibroids in the name of Jesus. I cancel anything that has connected to me that is not from you. I call forth your giant warrior Angels to surround and protect me. As your war club and weapons of war, I break down, undam and blow up all walls of protection around all witches, wizards, warlocks, satanist and the like and I break the power of every curse, hex, vex, spell, psychic prayer, psychic chain, all witchcraft, sorcery, magic. I cancel every plot and ploy of the enemy. I cancel all manipulation, mind control, jealousy, envy, new age tactics and anything hidden in secret places only you can see. I send every word curse and demon back to the sender 1000-fold and bind it to them by the blood of Jesus. Every snare and trap they set up for me, may they fall in it themselves. Father I pray they repent of their sins to turn their hearts away from evil and back to you Lord. I pray for a stress-free pain free pregnancy and delivery in Jesus's name.

Father I thank you for deliverance of my own sins, and I pray for your forgiveness for all the things I've said or done to attract opposition into my life. Cleanse and correct me Father. I am an open and willing vessel. Pour Lord. Heal me Father. Give me my son as you promised. Your word says in John 14:14 if I ask you anything in Your name, You will do it. Lord, I ask you for removal any foreign objects in my womb and to replace them with my son. If there is something I need to do or somewhere I need to go to make this happen show me. I'm not afraid of work, I just want to make sure the work I am doing is where You want me to do it. Lord protect me from empty labor. Keep me close to You, so close I can hear Your whisper. Holy Spirit order my steps, lead me, guide me. Father I don't want to miss what You have for me. I'm Yours. I thank You for answering my prayers. I thank You for restoring my health. I thank You for repairing my marriage. I pray You protect my husband, heal his heart in the broken places only you can see. I thank You for protecting my daughter and covering my family. I pray she only has interest and acts on the things that are of You. If it's not from You Lord, I don't want it and I pray You keep it away from my family. In Jesus' name, Amen.

I'd then talk to my son calling him out by his name and telling him what life will be like when he arrives and how amazing he will be.

Aiden, my sweet baby boy, mommy loves you so much. I can't wait for you to get here; it's going to be so much fun. We're going to go on ice cream dates and run and play all the time. You're going to play so many sports and I'm going to be your biggest fan. Mommy is going to give you so many cuddles and kisses. I'll read and sing to you daily; we'll even make up our own songs. We will laugh and have the best time together. You will be so handsome and full of integrity, people from all over the world are going to know you. You will be a leader of leaders, strong and very successful in everything you do. I know you're ready. I know you can hear me too. You're going to be with Jesus just for a little while longer. It won't be long now. You will be in my arms in no time! First, you're going to be in my tummy. You're going to be super healthy and stay in there the whole time until God says you're ready. You're going to have perfect hair, eyes, nose, hands, fingers and toes. I plead the blood of Jesus over every vein in your body. Your toes, feet, ankles, every joint, knees arteries, fingers, hands, knuckles, your legs will be strong to walk boldly in your purpose and glorifying God. Your arms, elbows and shoulders will stretch high in praise. Your neck, face, lips, teeth, cheeks, ears, eyes, nose, brain, skull will function for greatness. I plead the blood of Jesus over your kidneys, pancreas, liver, stomach, and lungs. Your heart will beat with power. Your hair will grow thick, curly and long. Your smile will light up every room. Your laugh will shift atmospheres. When you speak people will stop in their tracks to listen. You are a warrior for Christ, a generational shifter, prophetic voice and intuitive listener. You have a heart for God and His people. You speak with conviction, holding yourself and other accountable. You ooze with love and affection. You're noble, caring, loving, a scholar and excellent student of life. You're so awesome! Mommy loves you with every breath in my body. I give you to the Lord. I will follow His lead with raising you. You will yield to His voice you hear through me. You are perfect and more than what I've prayed for. You have my heart for eternity. In Jesus's name, Amen.

I did this first thing every single morning, every single day. Each day was a little different but the outline was the same. Gratitude. Warfare. Grace. Faith Activated.

I taught a series back in February called Activate Your Faith. That's all I heard the Lord say to me.

Activate your faith daughter.

The only way I know how to do that is with my words and my work. Doing all that I know I can in the natural so God can add His Super to it. One morning when I was praying, I felt a sharp pain on the left side of my stomach. It was so sharp I stopped mid-prayer to yell:

"Something just happened. Jesus, I don't know what you just did but I do know it was something!"

Once this moment happened, I began praying multiple times a day.

Chapter 8

I DON'T SEE ANYTHING

August 9th – Visit Jenn

My best friend Jenn was in the hospital on bed rest. Her baby boy was trying to come a few months early and they were keeping her so he'd stay in longer. She couldn't have any pressure on her pelvic area, she had to sit for showers and only could walk to the restroom and her bed. She planned a baby shower, but had to cancel it because she was in the hospital. Her birth plan was to have a C-section so I made sure to go to the hospital and spend some time with her. I picked up cupcakes and snacks on the way. I get to the parking garage and my ticket number was 303102. Remove the zeros, add the 1+2 and that's 333, my number and another breadcrumb from Jesus that I'm on His path for me.

I've been asked often about numbers. People see 222, 111, 11:11 and feel that it means something to them. I'm not a numerologist and I don't study horoscopes nor anything similar so I don't know what they may mean to you. I didn't know 3:33am was the time I was born until I was preparing for the first Straight Talk Woman Talk Intensive in Houston January

2016 and my mom found my birth certificate and told me. I was 35 years old. I didn't draw a connection to the number 3 until 2009. I remember attending church and wanting to sow a seed during offering time. All I had was 3 one-dollar bills; that's it, $3.00 to my name. The spirit was heavy and I felt the urge to give it all. One dollar for the Father, one dollar for the Son and one dollar for the Holy Spirit. I even told that to the person sitting next to me! I prayed for God to increase it 100-fold just like His word says in *Genesis 26:12*

> *Then Isaac sowed in that land, and received in the same year a hundredfold: and the Lord blessed him.*

The next day I went to check the mail at the mailboxes connected to the side of my apartment complex's office. When I opened the mailbox there was a tan bubble mailer in it, like the ones you'd use to put a CD (compact disc) in for safe shipping. It was addressed to me, but there was no return address on it so I didn't know who it was from. There was a trash cash by the mailbox I'd always use to throw out magazines and since I didn't know what this package was, I was prepared to toss it as well. I'm glad I opened it first, because inside it were 3, crisp, one-hundred-dollar bills folded in half! I immediately remember my seed the day before and shouted *God, you literally folded them*! I went inside the apartment complex office and asked the ladies if they opened my mailbox for anyone and they all said no it was the normal USPS – United State Postal Service person. I was blown away.

From that day on I paid close attention anytime I saw the number 3. I noticed a pattern of transition and connection to things that lead me closer to God when I saw it, so it became a prompt for me to pray and thank Him for whatever it is He is doing for and through me. As my relationship with Him grew so did my sensitivity to when He spoke to me. I can find the number 3 in anything He sends to me. It's gotten to the point where people I am connected to also stop to pray or send me pictures and screenshots when they see 333.

We think when God speaks it's a loud thunder, and while He can and does speak in that way, He more commonly whispers. Many times when we're talking to ourselves and thinking through our thoughts it's Him. The ah-ha moments when we suddenly get an idea or understanding about something isn't us but the Holy Spirit dropping breadcrumbs for us to follow. The only way to hear a whisper is to have your ear close to the lips of the person speaking. The closer you are to God, the clearer you can hear.

My visit with Jenn goes great. We laugh and pray; she's laying there all cute and round. I put her in the wheel chair and we take a stroll around the hospital and through the garden. It was so peaceful for us both. She knew her baby boy was coming soon, and I felt closer to mine.

Faith activated.

August 16th – Tornado Dream

I had a dream I was in the car with my Husband and another female. We were at the home of another woman who was trying to harm us. When we left we were driving down a two-lane highway surrounded by green pastures and crops for planting fruits and vegetables. The sky got eerie like it would in a place like Kansas when a tornado is coming. Then the wind got high, just like it would during a tornado, but instead of a tornado in the sky there was a large John Deere lawn mower that's used to cut crops flying in the air. It was cutting grass in the air with other cars attached to the back of it like a centipede or long string. It was a tornado but a wiggly one versus a circular one. We pulled over to the side of the road where the other bystanders were to look at it from across the street. Then it crashed in the pastures. Suddenly, the woman from the house we left walked up to our car to get a bag that was hers out our trunk. As she turned and walked away, she disappeared.

My alarm wakes me up. I wrote the dream down and prayed, asking God to reveal more to me about that dream. The tornado felt very real, my heart beat elevated and I felt I was on guard. I did some asking around and learned that tornado dreams represent an emotionally volatile or sensitive situation like an emotional storm. A sudden argument, conflict or unsettling experience. That was confirmed when later that day we had another Peninnah experience. What happened this time was very extreme and would normally make me angry, but I'd already released my emotions because of the dream. God used the dream to prepare me for what was going to happen later. I'd already taken control of my emotions so I didn't get as upset or bothered by what she did. I shared the dream with my Husband so we both knew how to handle and control the situation.

Entitlement is a drug that can be easily addictive. Jealously and envy are very dark spirits that can leave you so bitter you began to draw floods of negativity into your life. It bleeds into every relationship you have making it impossible to have a healthy one. The spirit of Peninnah is one that can affect any family member. The jealous cousin, negative aunt, disrespectful uncle or grandmother. It represents a person who loves to provoke you, highlight your short comings and see you fail. With the right mindset and relationship with God you can rise above it.

Prophetic dreams are real. They are bold and creative ways God communicates and confirms His word. When we're sleep our conscious mind is off, so everything is subconscious. Sub means below, conscious means aware and responding. When your subconscious is activated, you are operating below awareness and response. You can't over think what's happening, it just happens and its real. I believe God uses this time because there is no noise. There's nothing to distract or distort the message. That's why if I don't write down the dream when I wake, a lot of times I won't always remember it how it was. Once you are awake your conscious mind is activated and the noise distorts the intended message. We know in part and prophesy in part. He will use random things that don't make sense in the dream but have relevance to your life so you can later make sense of it. He'll use movies you've watched, books you've read, music you listen to, other people, animals; all which seem irrelevant, but give you grounding for interpretation.

The same day the tornado dream and Peninnah encounter happens, I get a call from my doctor's office. I didn't want to answer because they canceled my appointment in July and I was handling all the drama with Peninnah. Nevertheless, I picked up.

> Dr. Office: *Hello Mrs. Wilkins we're calling you to confirm your appointment on Monday.*
>
> Me: *I don't have an appointment. The last time we spoke was in July when you cancelled on me.*
>
> Dr. Office: *Well, we have you down, do you want to keep it?*

I say Ok and hang up the phone thinking to myself. *Jesus, did you really have these people set this appointment?* I yelled out to my Husband, *Baby the doctor just called to confirm the appointment I didn't make.*

> Him: *Who set it?*
>
> Me: *Jesus!*
>
> Him: *Sha-baa!! Look at God. Good for you. Now go get me my son!*
>
> Me: *He's been ordered and on the way!*

God had been so bold in developing me prophetically, I was very sensitive to His hand in something, so it changed my perspective about going to the doctor. I didn't make the appointment, but they called to confirm one. That's a God moment. God moments can't be explained nor do they make sense. He'd been nudging me all week to book an appointment. That call was my confirmation that time was of the essence. Not Chronos - our time that we measure in seconds and minutes on a clock, but Kairos, an appointed opportune moment which is how Gods' time operates. He's not subject to our time, He's the Author of it so time is subject to Him. This one moment was confirmation it was my time.

August 19th – Miracles

I woke up that Monday excited about my appointment. During my prayer time I focused heavily on God healing me of fibroids. I get to my doctor's office and immediately cry when I walk inside. She moved to a new location which was in a building next to the one where my best friend Jenn had just given birth to her son. The new office was on the 8th floor and the number eight means new beginnings. So, as I sit there, I'm thanking God for a new beginning. They walk me to exam room number 3 and I immediately fill with expectation. I give my doctor the cliff notes version of what's been happening since my last visit in 2017 and told her I'm ready to try again for a baby, but I wanted to do IVF. She gives me a normal check-up and tells me I have a lump in my right breast that she wants me to get checked out. I say to myself *really Jesus, cancer too? Lord please, I need a break.*

She sends me down the hall to do an ultra-sound to check on my fibroids. As I walk to the ultra-sound room, I'm praying in the spirit and asking the Lord to give me strength and good news. It's a vaginal ultra-sound so I undress from the waist down and lay on the bed. I said to myself, *God is about to do something. I can feel it.* The ultra-sound technician is really nice. She tells me: *I'm going to be quick, just want to get a quick look at your fibroids.* I close my eyes and began praying in the spirit. She's moving the camera around and a few minutes pass by when she asks:

How many did you say you had?

Me: *two, lemon sized.*

Nurse: *Are you sure?*

Me: *Yes! I still have the ultra-sound picture of them.*

Nurse: *Really? Because I don't see anything.*

I start laughing and crying, then she turns the monitor to me and there it was; my uterus, clear, beautiful and fibroid free! Not one scar! I yell, *that's God!* After major surgery to remove multiple grapefruit sized fibroids and two coming back, my uterus looked as perfect as it did the day God formed me in my mother's womb. I get dressed while she tells my doctor. The whole office shuts down to review my chart. I go back to exam room 3 and begin to dig through my phone for the picture of the ultra-sound from the two fibroids that returned in 2017. My doctor comes in and is in shock. She says she's never seen this happen before in 25 years of doing myomectomies. She asked me what happened? My response, *God happened.* Then she shares with tears in her eyes:

> *I don't know what it is about today. There was a woman in this same room I saw this morning. She had an issue with bleeding and I was supposed to do surgery on her today. She told me that the spirit told her I won't be able to do it because she was healed. When I went to check her, she was! Nothing was wrong.*

I'm crying like a baby at this point. I said, she was my Angel clearing the path for my miracle today. She said:

I don't have your old chart because we moved. Do you have the ultra-sound picture? I need to show my dad. He's a believer in Christ and he prayed over my office before I moved in. He told me God told him I'd witness more miracles than I'd ever seen before. I want to share your story with him.

I'm shaking and my eyes are blurry from my tears, so I can barely focus on finding the fibroid ultra-sound picture. I later found and emailed it to her. She tells me to go do IVF immediately, then gives me instructions to have a mammogram done. I walk out her office and Facetime my Husband in the hallway to tell him the incredible news. He hit me with a few *shucks*, and *sha-baas* and couple of *shondos*. Those of you who know my Husband know exactly what I'm talking about. He was fired up and extremely encouraging. As we're talking about the appointment, I get revelation.

The ultrasound tech only works on Mondays. The appointment they canceled in July was on a Wednesday. Had I gone I would've gotten the news about the lump in my breast without knowing the fibroids were gone. God knew I would've swore off doctors again had that happened, so what I considered devastating with a canceled doctor visit was simply a detour!

I get inside my car and immediately begin to make calls to all the women the Holy Spirit told me to share the ocean dream with and a few additional ones. Here's a timeline of the calls I made that week in August.

20th –

- Called Toni, Shannon, Arianna, Garlinda, and Andrea.

- Andrea said my intercession for my family wasn't just for me. Chains broke in the spirit for many others.

21st –

- Called Dr. Alexis. Her husband had a prophetic dream and said for her to not go through with the fibroid removal surgery she had planned that week, she prayed for God to show her someone who has had a miraculous removal of fibroids. 20 minutes later I called her while on my way home from the doctor to tell her about my miracle. She cancelled her surgery.
- Another Kingdom sister had a doctor's appointment the day before to discuss fertility. I didn't know she was trying to conceive, I just called her as God told me to.
- Another one didn't want any more children, they were happy with one son, but when I called her to share my testimony, she told me about her battle with endometriosis. We'd known each other since 2011, had tons of double dates and play dates with our kids, but I never knew what she was battling. I added her to my prayer list for healing.

22nd –

- Jenn has baby boy vaginally, a complete restoration from the stillborn she had to deliver vaginally years prior. *Isaiah 61:3 To appoint unto them that mourn in Zion, to give unto them beauty for ashes, the oil of joy for mourning, the garment of praise for the spirit of heaviness; that they might be called trees of righteousness, the planting of the Lord, that he might be glorified.*

- Called Dr. Kimberly, who has shared on Straight Talk Woman Talk many times, she also referenced Hannah as well, and said *God isn't done yet, there's more to the story.*
- Called Dr. Estrelita, who was the very first-person God told me to have share on Straight Talk Woman Talk in 2015. I told her God told me she and her Husband will have another baby.
- I called Pinky in South Africa, who I hadn't talked to in a year. We met through business, and it was her church I was at when God told me His daughters are hungry. When I did the Straight Talk Woman Talk Intensive there in 2018 she and her sister led praise and worship. Soon as I'm done sharing my testimony and tell her that the Lord showed me she will have a baby too, she stood up and showed me a super pregnant tummy. I parked my truck in the Best Buy parking lot and ran around it like a crazy woman. She then tells me she put a prayer she wrote for me in her prayer box. She went home and sent me a video of her opening it. It was glued shut so her husband had to help her. She wrote:

Porshea Wilkins-Agomo to be pregnant with a healthy son in 2018. To carry baby full term and have a happy marriage. Dated: 15 December 2017. In the name of Jesus. Thank you, Lord, for answering my prayer.

- Called Rachel who I hadn't spoken to in a few years. She and her husband at the time were trying to conceive, but discovered after years of fertility tests on her, that he wasn't producing enough sperm. She'd since adopted, and said my call was confirmation from conversation with friend day before. I told her she will carry as well and to name her baby and begin to call them forth as I did.

24th –

- Called Arin who partnered with me for Straight Talk Woman Talk Intensive in South Africa just as Pinky did. Arin's husband told her something that hit like a ton of bricks with revelation:

Water doesn't flow through a pipe without the pipe getting wet.

Everything she witnessed and participated in happening for others would happen for her. After my call her faith was activated and she began the IVF process again.

- Called Earlisha – She'd just left her grandmother's funeral. I shared my testimony and told her that her sister who also struggles with infertility will get pregnant again. Earlisha had ectopic pregnancies (fertilized egg implants outside the uterus). She hadn't been to the doctor since her last ectopic pregnancy, which was the night before the Straight Talk Woman Talk Intensive in Houston January 2016. She was going to play a big part in the event, her testimony was so powerful, but instead she was admitted into the hospital. After my call she scheduled a doctor's appointment.
- Called Anotinette – I attended her Pretty Petals conference as a speaker the year prior. While there, I planted my prayer for my son in her prayer box. When I called to tell her about my miracle, I told her she will be getting married and having a baby soon. She shared she just reconnected with an ex-boyfriend of eleven years, who wrote her name down as his wife. Her twin sister had been struggling with infertility as well.

- Update 2020: Antoinette's sister give birth to a baby girl. 2021: Antoinette is officially married to the former boyfriend she told me she reconnected with.

26th –

- Called Quiana. I met her through our Husbands in 2015. Their son Landon was six months old and the first baby boy my Husband and I had to love on. Their daughter Laila and our daughter became best friends. She shared a video testimony for the first Straight Talk Woman Talk Intensive in Houston January 2016. I hadn't talked to her in a long time, so I sent her a text telling her I have a Word from the Lord to share. After sharing my testimony update, I told her they will have another boy. They got pregnant in 2020 and miscarried, but kept their faith, and in 2021 conceived and delivered a healthy, handsome baby boy named Lex Gavin which means Warrior of God.

After I called everyone, I called Jenn to tell her the news and to get her IVF doctors information to make an appointment.

August 28th – IVF appointment + Miracle

My cycle was late but my pregnancy test was negative so I still went to the IVF appointment. Hubby and I get to the office building and look up the office number for the IVF doctor. We see he's on the 3rd floor and its Wednesday the 3rd day of the week so immediately get excited. I check in and they place me in exam room 3. I'm extra excited. They draw my blood and get a semen sample from my husband. I finally do my mammogram.

September 3rd – Second IVF appointment

The day started out horrible. My husband was supposed to go with me to the appointment, but he was at the bank when it was time for us to leave so I had to go by myself. He said he didn't know I needed him. I'm hotter than a fire cracker at him because if anyone knows how important this was it's him. He was having a Mars moment for sure. I'm crying and talking all manners of trash to myself about him while driving there. I really disliked him in that moment. Then he had the nerve to show up smiling and being nice - so annoying. Made me even more mad. So, we're sitting in the lobby of the IVF doctor a mess.

They call us in the back to discuss the results. My blood is good and he had super sperm so we were good to go, the doctor wanted to check my uterus to make sure it was healthy for implantation. I'm still upset with my Husband, but tried to compartmentalize enough to get through this procedure. Anxiety sets in because it's a male doctor, and no man had seen my lady parts since I started dating my Husband. I was also anxious because I wasn't 100% certain IVF was the route God wanted me to take. The doctor said it should take him a few seconds to check everything and it wouldn't hurt. He begins to check and I feel pressure, followed by scratching, then more pressure. I can feel his frustration. I start hyperventilating and crying. I know something is wrong.

Doctor: *I can't get through your cervix.*

Me: *What do you mean?*

Doctor: I can't get it through, its resisting.

I yell: *Stop! Stop! Stop! Please. Don't do anything else!!*

My Husband was trying his best to comfort me, I believe it was in that moment he realized why I was so upset when he thought I wouldn't need him there. We meet with the doctor afterwards and he explains that my cervix is sealed shut from scar tissue. I had a leap done in 2004 when I lived in Ohio to remove potentially cancerous cells. They told me I'd have problems dilating and would more than likely need to have a C-section to give birth.

The IVF doctor told me he never had that happen before. The utensil he used was thinner than a stick pen and rubber so it should've taken a few seconds, but every time he tried to enter my cervix something pushed it out. I leave there again swearing off doctors and anything extra, choosing to just stand in faith. I got my anointing oil from the 2018 event with Apostle Boyd, poured some in my bubble bath then prayed over myself and my Husband. As I sat in the tub I heard the Holy Spirit say:

I closed your cervical wall to close that door.

He showed me the hand of God at my cervical wall blocking the doctor. I hear Him say:

You're not infertile daughter, you're just not in timing.

I cried. After my bath I felt so encouraged, I checked the mail on the kitchen counter and saw there was a letter from the mammogram place. I figured I'd go ahead and get whatever the news was going to be, out the way. I added healing for my breasts like my fibroids to my morning prayer the moment I got the news I had a lump, so I was at peace with whatever the results were going to be. I looked at the letter and not only did the results come back negative for cancer, it said there was no lump! God did it - again.

In that moment I knew without a doubt I would conceive naturally. I longed for that feeling of certainty and confirmation; it felt good to know that I was hearing God correctly when it came to how I'd conceive, it left me wondering though why He would send me down that path if that wasn't how He was going to do it. Everything God does is principled. Principles are laws, they aren't subject to emotion or condition. You sow, you reap. There's a part we play in the process and when we honor it, He acts. When we ask for a miracle, He always gives an instruction. What happens next is contingent upon our obedience to the instruction. I've learned over time that you must participate in your own rescue.

That night my Husband and I made love with no thought of a baby. For the first time in a long time, it was just he and I enjoying and loving on each other as Husband and Wife.

November – Holiday Headache

I kept getting negative ovulation test results on both the manual ones you dip in urine and the digital ones, so I threw them out and downloaded the Flo period tracker to see if I could target my ovulation day better with that. It said my peek ovulation day was the Monday before Thanksgiving. I was extremely tired that week but still looking forward to my favorite holiday. Both the Nigerians and Americans primarily from my Husband's side of the family, were coming that year, well over fifty people.

I learned how to cook from my grandmother; no recipes, I just flow by smell, feel and sight, while my grandmother Martha Evelyn "Zip" Hicks, comes down from Heaven to whisper in my ear what to do. Nothing but soul! I even created a blog called The Wilkins Kitchen where I'd share my creations from time to time. I planned my menu and had a full feast outlined all from scratch; turkey, ham, dressing, mac and cheese, collard greens, peach cobbler the works! No pies other than the cobbler because I cook, I don't bake. Baking requires measurements while cooking doesn't. I do however, plan to perfect my grandmothers caramel cake one day! Jesus himself would come eat that with us growing up! It was full of glory!

The Thanksgiving prior in 2018 was very stressful for me. Two days before the holiday, my Husband and I returned from a business trip in Florida. I immediately began cooking when I walked in the house, I was only cooking for the four people in my home so it wasn't going to take long at all. The night before Thanksgiving, around 9:00pm, just as I'm cleaning the kitchen and laying out the plates for the next day, my Husband gets a call from his uncle, a Nigerian Chief, asking what time should the Nigerians arrive.

I love them all, they've always been very welcoming to me, especially Uncle Bikey, he's the glue of the family and the most thoughtful and caring. He's also an Ophthalmologists; an extremely respected and connected one at that, which comes in handy when we need something medial done. I love Nigerian culture and the community my Husbands' family has created. Lots of dancing, games and loud debates about current events.

The phone is on speaker so I can hear their conversation. As they begin to talk about Thanksgiving, I have no doubt my beloved Husband is going to tell his uncle I'm tired and already finished cooking for four people in my home, so we're not doing anything for the big family. Instead, he yells from the living room:

Baby what time should they be here?

My blood began to boil hotter than the pasta water for my macaroni. I gave him the look of death and he had the nerve to shrug his shoulders like he didn't know what to say or what was going on. We were just around hundreds of people for business and all I was talking about the entire week was how excited I was to sit on my couch and relax for Thanksgiving! I'm an introvert, I like my peace and my space. I socialize in spurts and can be extroverted, but when I'm done, I need time to reset.

He put me on the spot with his uncle, so I either had to be the unfriendly American wife and tell them they can't come or the welcoming one and stress myself out. I choose to be the welcoming one which meant I had to go back to the grocery store at 11:00pm the night before Thanksgiving to get more food, because I only prepared for the four that live in my home - like I'd been saying all week.

I finally finished cooking at 3:00am. I get to bed and my Husband is fast asleep snoring while I laid there crying from exhaustion and disappointment in myself for not making the choice that created peace for me. The Nigerians were hosting Holiday's a certain way for years, taking turns at designated homes. I attended a few Christmas and New Year's gatherings, but I didn't know their history around it. The expectation was for everyone in the family to attend all Holiday gatherings like Thanksgiving, Christmas, New Years and 4th of July. Anyone who knows Nigerians know that culturally they run deep in packs and are always late. My family and I are the exact opposite.

My Husband was the eldest son of their eldest sister, and had an American Wife so he was given the hosting duties for Thanksgiving, which is why his uncle called. The problem was that nobody told me anything about this transfer or asked if I wanted to do it. I cook for Thanksgiving and celebrate it because I always have since I was a little girl, preparing a feast for an army is completely different. It ended up going well that year, with only five or so additional people, but I was still exhausted.

When Thanksgiving 2019 came around and my Husband asked this time if I was up for cooking for everyone, I agreed because we'd just moved into our new home and I was fully refreshed. The new house was much bigger than the previous one we got married in. I had a beautiful kitchen as well as a decked-out patio with a grill and large backyard overlooking the lake that's great for entertaining. So, I began to plan. In my family everyone pitches in for any function we decide to get together for. We all either cook together or bring something to help with the day. No one shows up empty handed and if they do, they help clean up afterwards. We set a time to sit and eat as a family, then relax afterwards to watch football, have dessert, play games and take naps. Showing up after the designated time to eat is disrespectful. It throws off the flow of the day because someone has to get up and walk you through the menu and serving or clean up again.

I sent his family the list of what I needed them to bring, and to my surprise some of the elders were offended. I received a phone call by one of them designed to get me in order. I wasn't going to set myself up for another disappointment or night of tears like the year prior, so I stood firm on my position; needless to say, that call didn't go as they expected.

There were lots of rules they were trying to impose on me, which didn't work because you can't tell me how to run anything at my house - I don't care who you are. Especially for something that I'm doing all the work and paying for. I was upset with my Husband for allowing it to happen, considering what I experienced the year prior, I wanted peace! I already told him how it was going to go and instead of shutting them down for me as my Husband, he played more to their side as the nephew. He even knew they were going to call me, but didn't tell me. He was upset with my response because it created tension with him and them. I was extremely mad and ready to cancel the whole thing! This is supposed to be a happy time for me to cook with my grandmother in my ear and my Jazz music playing in my beautiful new kitchen, not a time to have a face-off with your family about what they, as guests, are going to try to do in my house.

Thanksgiving was my favorite Holiday and I was now dreading the thought of it. It was a clash of cultures for sure. I just wanted the day to hurry up and come, so it could hurry up and be over. I let him know that will be the last time I cook for everyone like that. I was upset. I knew it wasn't going to be the last time, it would just be a few more years before I do it again. Even then I'll cater it versus cook it! Thankfully my mother and aunt were there to help manage everything and clean up. My mother-in-law brought a cooler of jollof rice and drinks, my father-in-law and a few others brought desserts, so we had everyone covered.

Thanksgiving Day comes, I got a few hours of sleep the night prior so I didn't care what I looked like, I threw on a random wig and put a few strokes of color on my eyebrows. Our house is full of people, I'm completely exhausted and my feet are swollen. We were scheduled to eat at 1:00p. Those who were there on time ate with us, the rest showed up late and on through the evening. While they loved the food, most didn't even know I cooked it. I didn't feel appreciated at all. I felt used, like I was the maid or the help. I fixed my plate, ate and took a nap on the couch with everyone still there. One woman, who was pregnant, came inside and prayed for me. I didn't know her and was too tired to get to know her or discern anything, but she was sweet and my mother-in-law brought her to me so I let her pray. I didn't even get up to greet her. It was rude, but I was wore out. The only thing I had the energy to do was sit. I'd later see she was onto something big.

I love small, relaxed gatherings of ten or less people. That's why I'm surprised God even chose me for ministry. He knows how I feel about crowds of people. I only speak when He gives me something to say. I could have a whole schedule planned with marketing and everything and if He said sit down, I'll cancel it all in a heartbeat, unbothered by what it looks like to anyone else. Ministry is about salvation. You're dealing with people's souls. Not to mention their demons too! You can't show up to that assignment un-prepared. You'll lead people astray and risk taking all manners of mess home to your family and not even know it. I do it out of obedience; even this book. I was Ok with it just being a short prayer guide, but here we are. The Holy Spirit jumped in the mix and now you're getting all my business and a witness to my blessings.

Chapter 9

PROMISE KEPT

December 2019 – Putting Pressure

I was still recovering from Thanksgiving and praying every morning, but now I'm adding pressure.

> *Father, the year is almost up, I've been fighting, praying, believing and working for this child you promised me. What am I missing? What do you want me to do? At this point you're gonna have to just come sit right here and tell me because I'm not catching any signs. Please don't let me go into a new year with the same problem. I've taken care of everyone else's child, loving them as my own, I've even prayed over the wombs of your daughters and they conceived, but now is my turn. I want to carry my own.*

My Husband was taking a trip to Vegas on the 13th to watch a boxing match with his best friend. I was happy to have the house to myself and watch HGTV with a glass of wine Kool-Aid (that's what I call Moscato since its super sweet and barely any alcohol) and relax. My cycle was scheduled to come on the

12th but didn't. I wasn't excited because it skipped a few days many times in the past, and I'd take a test thinking I was late and pregnant, but the test would be negative and immediately after my cycle would come. I wasn't going to set myself up for another let down so I decided to wait a couple of days.

December 14th comes and still no menstrual cycle. I call my Husband to tell him I'm 3 days late. He was scheduled to be home Sunday the 15th, and I wasn't going to do anything until he returned. I told him I was going to wait until Monday the 16th to take a pregnancy test. I was giving my cycle time to skip if that's what it was doing. Sunday comes, my husband is home and still no cycle, discharge or anything that would normally let me know it was coming. I had two digital pregnancy tests in the restroom. Hubby and I are on the couch watching one of our shows, talking about his trip and what time I'd take the test on Monday. I had so much anticipation I couldn't wait anymore, when the clock hit mid-night Monday December 16th I got off the couch and told him let's go ahead and do it. I told him it's gonna be what it's gonna be, dragging it out is just going to stress me out and make the process worse. I had to rip it off like a band aide!

I get to the restroom and decided this time to pee in a cup versus on the stick. I pee, dip in the stick for five minutes, sit the test down on the counter, then read the instructions. It said to dip it for twenty-five seconds. I only dipped for five seconds. Crap! I'm thinking I ruined the test and will have to take another. I grab the water sitting on the sink to drink, closed the door to the toilet room and sit waiting to pee again. Nothing comes out so I get up and as I walk out the toilet room into the main restroom, my timer goes off.

The 3-minute wait is over.

I walk to my restroom counter.

Nnamdi heard me come out the toilet room so he walks into restroom and asks, *Ok, where are we?*

I look at the test and for the first time in five years it said in bold letters:

PREGNANT.

We shouted, hugged and kissed then looked at each other like we didn't know what to do next. He told me he felt vindicated because having this experience with his wife was in alignment with God's will and an experience he always longed for since he received the prophecy decades sooner. We go to my mom's room to tell her the news, she gets excited but is half asleep. The next day I call my doctor to tell her I have a positive pregnancy test, they schedule me to come in right away. My mom comes into the living room and asks if I told her I was pregnant last night because she didn't know if that was a dream or not. We told her yes and she jumped with joy! Just a few inches off the ground though because her knees are special.

Once at the Doctor I take a pregnancy test and it's positive. They put me in exam room 3 again, I sang and praised God the whole time I waited. I hadn't seen my doctor since the fibroid removal miracle, so she comes inside the room with a big smile on her face excited to see me.

Dr: *So how was the IVF experience?*

Me: *I didn't do it.*

Dr: *What?! You got pregnant naturally?!*

Me: *Yes!*

Dr: *How?*

Me: *I prayed!*

Dr: *No way! Can you pray for the world!? We need your power!*

She said it was too soon to check anything on the ultrasound and for me to come back in a couple of weeks. I text and called the ladies who God had me share the fibroid removal miracle. When I told Dr. K. Ellison I was blown away:

> Dr. K: *Girllll I have no words just praise! Lisssssssssssssssssennn! Never stop praying and believing. Congratulations! Praying and excited to share with my prayer family of intercessors who've been praying as well. Check out this text from one of the intercessors. We've been petitioning Heaven for 3 couples... you and Jarrod are one... she just asked about you all on December 11th... see screenshot:*

> Lady O: *Good morning Dr. Kimberly, How are Salena and Mombe, Porshea and Jarrod and Leslie and John doing in conceiving? One of these couples are pregnant how are they?*

> Dr. K: *Good Morning Lady Orr! John and Leslie say they are about 7 months. Sirleena and Nnamdi, Porshea and Jarrod no word just yet.*

I thank God for all His sons and daughters who stand on their post interceding on our behalf! Our purpose is to do what He calls us to do so He can fulfill His purpose. It's a chain reaction. A ripple effect in the Spirit. Like a choir singing a song; altos, sopranos, bass, tenors, drums, organ, piano, trombone all have a different tune at a different time and when on their post they shift the atmosphere together! Christmas Day comes, I'm so happy and filled with expectation and love. As I'm sitting on my couch thanking God for keeping His promise I hear Him say again:

> *You weren't infertile my daughter, you just weren't in-timing.*

I don't know about you, but every time I hear that phrase it does something to me. That Word was given to me twice in 2019 but it is for you right now! My sister, God loves you and keeps His promises, just stay on your post so you can be in alignment with His timing. Though it tarry, wait. Keep your faith activated. It will surely come. It doesn't matter your age or your medical status. God doesn't yield to science especially when He created all the scientists and gave them the gifts to practice the science that they do! Do you know He's giving babies to women who have had hysterectomies? There is nothing, not-one-thing that He cannot do!

January 6, 2020 – Beats Of Love

We go to the doctor for our ultra sound to hear Aiden's heartbeat for the first time (I shared that video in my Supernatural

Pregnancy Docuseries on my website StraightTalkWoman-Talk.com so make sure you watch it, it's the movie version of this book). The same nurse who witnessed the fibroid miracle was there to do this ultra sound as well. She inserts the tube, turns on the big monitor on the wall, increases the volume and we hear the sweetest sound coming from the cutest little chicken nugget! *Boop boop! Boop boop!* I cried.

As she's walking me through the ultra-sound she begins to talk about my ovaries, and says something that jumps out to me.

> *The egg came from the left ovary and that's where he implanted, on the left side.*

The Holy Spirit immediately brings to my remembrance the morning I was praying and felt a sharp pain on my left side. I remember it was so sharp I stopped mid-prayer to yell from the pain. I knew and said in that moment that something happened. It wasn't just the fibroids that were removed, it was everything! She confirmed it. God was cleansing out and healing whatever needed to be healed on that side to make way for the egg to be fertilized. Isn't that amazing? That's why you can't tell me God isn't real. I know science is important, but it's done by people. People are not miraculous. The way God uses us to execute His purpose is the miraculous.

People have power, but we're not Omnipotent and have all power, only God is. He has all the power imaginable and beyond spreading it to us as He sees fit! The moment you think you know it all and have all the answers, He throws a miracle in the mix to make you realize how much you truly don't know. Reminding you that no matter what, above all - He is still on the throne!

When we leave, I contact all the women I contacted before to share the news.

Pregnant During the Pandemic

I didn't want to tell everyone I was pregnant and was struggling with how I would hide it. Then the coronavirus pandemic hit and America had to shut down. This was like Heaven for introverts! The pandemic gave me a good reason to not have to explain to people why I wasn't showing up anywhere, it was perfect.

No one knew we were pregnant, not even our daughter. I was always sitting when she'd come out her room or something. Things weren't yet restored with her, she'd been very disobedient that year, which was very uncharacteristic of her. Once I got pregnant God had me rest from warfare. I prayed fervently for her every morning just as I prayed for the conception of my son. He said to rest and that's what I did. We gave her the option to come home with us only when she wanted.

It was extremely hard to not tell her, I cried many days because of it, but I trusted God. We knew her response wasn't going to be what it should've been because of the manipulation she'd been subjected to from Peninnah. When we did share it with her, I was already seven months. She was excited but hurt, although she never directly said it, her actions and comments from time to time would let us know she was upset because we kept it from her. We were prepared for that and after discussing with her why, she said she understood. Those conversations are never fun, but always necessary for growth. We knew restoration would take time and as she grows the seeds we've planted from years of feeding her the Word of

God and His principles of life, will eventually come to harvest. We're family forever and have a lifetime of love to stand with her through it all.

We kept our focus on all things peace and I had the absolute best pregnancy! Not a moment of sickness just as I asked in my daily prayer. Zero complications. No pain. Nothing. I had normal swelling from water retention, but that was it. I didn't have any crazy cravings. I was looking forward to eating chocolate and burgers every day, but I couldn't even stand the smell of it. Couldn't eat pizza either and I love pepperoni pizza! I craved salads and beef enchiladas. Every doctor's visit was like a waste of time because everything was perfect - his development, my health, everything. We could've handled the non-ultra sound visits over the phone! My Husband would go with me, but he couldn't come inside the Doctor's office so he'd sit in the lobby of the hospital or in the car in the garage and we'd jump on Zoom or Facetime so he could be there and see everything with me.

We only shared with a very short list and kept them all posted along the way. Some were concerned that I was keeping silent out of fear of losing the baby. I assured them that wasn't it. In a world where everyone runs online for everything first, I wanted to focus on being present in my pregnancy. This was a precious moment that I'd fought so hard for. Why would I share that with people who didn't actually know me? Why would I keep the people who prey and pray for my downfall updated? The online world is much bigger than my real world. It's easy to think the people online are your friends, but they are not. What is the extent of your relationship with them outside of the likes, comments and shares? For majority of us, it's nothing. There are people who I've met online and have a whole conversation with through comments, but can't find two words to say when I see them in person. Don't know their faces and I can't I remember their names. It's completely awkward. Those are not people who I'd share this with. They may feel like they know me because they've seen the progression of my relationship with my Husband, or consider me a mentor because they've listened to my teachings. Maybe we were in the same business together at one point, or went to the same church or something, but we never talked outside of that space.

Obviously everyone on social media isn't bad, and there's nothing wrong with using it. The key is to not make it your master allowing it to manipulate you into thinking you have to share everything. Share what you want, when you want, if you want, we are not entitled to your private life. My focus has always been to make sure the content posted in my real life is more viral than anything shared online. Social media is a marketing tool for the projects I work on, nothing more, nothing less. I'm intentional with what I share. Silence can be misinterpreted, but never misquoted, you have to grow to become 100% OK with letting whoever think whatever. Your promise is extremely fragile, everyone shouldn't be allowed access. Keeping my pregnancy close was the best decision ever. It was so peaceful I even stopped having dreams! God gave me a full reset and I enjoyed every bit.

July 2020 – Constipated or Contractions?

My due date was estimated to be around mid-August. Every time I went to the doctor it was different so we never really knew. During July my doctor appointments were weekly. I started feeling intense pressure in my pelvic area. No position was comfortable to sleep in, not even my rocking chair. I knew Aiden was ready to be born soon, he was head down now and I had so much discomfort. I didn't feel pretty, and wasn't interested at all in taking maternity pictures. I thought had nothing to wear, my hair was a mess, and I didn't know who would do my make up. Hubby convinced me to do it, so we could have it for memories. I called my friend and scheduled an appointment for her to do my crochet braids, told my friends De'el and Quiana I was ready for photos, Quiana said she'd get a mutual friend to come to the house to do my make-up so I didn't have to worry about doing it myself or leaving the house on that day. I had a beautiful tropical print dress I ordered a year prior from Instagram. I never wore it because I thought it was too small. It was a large, but super stretchy. I decided to try it on, to my surprise it fit perfectly! Hair, check! Make-up, check! Blue nails, check! Eye-brow wax, check! Outfit, check! 99% of my scrolling on Instagram is to look at cooking, creative and dream board stuff. I saved creative baby stuff over the years and saw a pregnancy announcement photo idea I really liked. I wanted to make custom printed blue shirts to wear as the announcement, Hubby and I came up with the design.

5 years.
9 months.
1 promise.
Our baby boy (with baby feet)

It took no time to make them. I ordered a pair of light denim maternity jeans from Target, that turned out to be the only maternity item I purchased, I wore sweat pants and pajamas my whole pregnancy. We took pictures July 20th and they came out better than amazing!

That whole week, I felt like I needed to poop but after sitting on the toilet forever nothing would happen. I thought I was constipated. Once I got to 38 weeks, the safe window for delivery, my visits were more frequent. I told my doctor about my constipation, she told me to eat cucumbers and take Dulcolax which is a gentle laxative. A couple of days later I go back to the doctor to tell her nothing changed. By this time, its July 29th, I'm 38 weeks and 4 days. Sitting hurts due to the pressure on my pelvic area and I'm extra uncomfortable. We do another ultra-sound and everything is perfect. She tells me to just keep taking the Dulcolax and it will happen.

I went to Target to pick up the Dulcolax and during the drive home my pelvic pain intensified. I have a high tolerance for pain, so it felt like a bad menstrual cramp and constipation mix versus contractions. I get home and read up on Braxton Hicks contractions, which did nothing but confuse me. Goggle can really be counterproductive at times. With so much information it's hard to miss the negative things that can mess with your mind.

By this time, it's around 3:00p and Jarrod comes back from the store with a birthday cake and flowers for my birthday the next day, July 30th. Our favorite cake is the white sheet cake from Kroger Grocery store. No other cake in the world is better – not even our wedding cake! We get all our celebration cakes from Kroger and eat it with Blue Bell Homemade Vanilla ice cream, the artificially flavored one, never vanilla bean! It's a Texas thing.

We put the cake in the fridge and go to the bedroom. Jarrod notices that I'm squeezing my butt cheeks when I walk and asked what was wrong, I told him it was the only way I could release the pressure on my pelvic area, which was intensifying. I call a few of our friends to tell him how I'm feeling. Both of the wives had given birth multiple times so I knew they could relate. I couldn't sit, it was too much pressure, so I leaned over the side of my bed while standing. I feel like the Dulcolax is starting to work so I go to the restroom. I sit and nothing happens, just a little tinkle of pee, but when I wiped, I noticed there was clear discharge on the tissue. I remembered reading about the mucus plug one night while googling about contractions. It's a potential indicator you're going into labor soon. We tell our friends we'll call them back so we can call the doctor. By now it's 4:00p. We tell our doctor what's going on and she says that's nothing to worry about, just relax and monitor it to see how I feel the next day.

A few minutes later I have to pee again, this time when I wiped I saw light pink, which means I was spotting. This was my first time seeing any kind of blood during my pregnancy. I yell and tell my husband, he yells *"Pack up we're going to the hospital!"* We call our doctor to tell her I was spotting and we want to go to the hospital. She gives us instructions on what to do. Takes us about 15 minutes to gather everything just in case they admit me. I was going to get a slice a cake before I left, but figured I'd be back in a few hours so I didn't.

The hospital was 35 minutes away and I felt every bump in the road. It was dark out and raining, so we take it easy on the drive, but still pushing to get there. I kept saying my whole pregnancy I didn't want any theatrics for delivery. I didn't want any water break or anything to happen anywhere but the hospital, no delivery in the car or any of that. I had no interest in being on the news for giving birth on the side of the road! I wanted a good ole normal hospital delivery. COVID-19 was still going around so we had to wear face masks everywhere, I hated them because I needed all the air I could get and the masks didn't help. We get to the hospital and thankfully they let both of us in, the last thing I wanted was to give birth without him. We get to the pre-delivery room and they test me for COVID which was negative as the Holy Spirit told me it would be. After connecting me to the monitors the nurse checks my cervix; no dilation, so she says my doctor will be in soon.

They give me some apple juice to perk up Aiden's heartbeat. He was always a chill baby. He only kicked when it was time to eat. My doctor comes in to check my cervix as well, still no dilation. After about 10 minutes or so the nurse comes back to share they are going to induce my labor. It would be a

12-hour process I'd do at the hospital. All I could think about was my cake at home! She then tries to check my cervix again and as she inserts her fingers I feel scratching. I yell for her to stop. She had long nails and I could feel every bit of them. I made her switch with the other nurse. About 20 minutes later the nurse comes back to let me know my doctor said we're going to do a C-Section at 12:00p tomorrow.

Me: But that's my birthday! I have cake at home!

Nurse: Well Happy Birthday you're having a baby!

My husband wanted Aiden to be born on his birthday. I wanted him to have his own day. God saw otherwise. By this time, it's after mid-night and they take us to my room. Thankfully my Husband was able to stay the whole time. COVID messed up a lot of birthing plans for a lot of families, many women had to be in the hospital alone and the father's missed the experience.

My contractions intensify at this point. It was as if Aiden knew what the doctor said. They gave me pain killers and I'd fall asleep off and on as I watched my husband sleep peacefully on the couch next to me.

Happy Birthday to Us

Here we are, Thursday July 30th my 39th birthday. 12:45pm comes and they wheel me down to the operating room. I'm excited but nervous. All I could think about was how I was dropped the last time, so this time I made sure to talk to everyone in the operating room before they touched me. My husband wasn't allowed in the operating room until they were getting ready to take Aiden out. As they wheeled me in, everyone was sharing who they were and their role, it was overwhelming. I needed them to slow down, so before they gave me any medicine or connected me to any machines, I told them all to stand in front of me to make eye contact. I shared with them what my previous experience was like at a different hospital. I told them I don't like surprises. *Don't do anything to me without telling me what you're going to do and what I can expect. If its pressure, say pressure. If its pain, say pain. Just don't let me find out after you do it, and if I ask a question, answer it. If I say something, pause and listen. Just because you may see me as a strong black woman don't assume I can handle whatever you do to me, treat me with the same care you would all the others.* They all agreed and did as I asked.

The male nurse who did my epidural was hilarious. He walked me through the whole process. He told me I may feel pain when he inserted the needle in my back, but I felt nothing. Once I lay back, he tells me they are about to put in the catheter, a flexible tube inserted through a narrow opening into a body cavity, particularly the bladder, for removing fluid. It was going to be inserted into my clitoris. I knew exactly what that was about because I had it done before without medication when I was in college. I got bit by a spider and they needed my urine. Instead of having me pee in a cup like a normal person they put in a catheter, it was extremely painful. He says jokingly, *this is the test to see if the epidural took or not. If you feel it, it ain't working!* We laughed and I wait. They announce it was in, I tell them I felt nothing and everyone cheered.

I don't know how much time passed before my Husband came in the room. I was heavily drugged up and super relaxed. I remember praying and asking God for a stress free, pain free delivery. He definitely came through! Hubby begins to record and repeat to me what they were saying. Then the male nurse says they are getting ready to take him out and I'm going to feel pressure on my chest. It didn't hurt at all, just felt like an adult sat on my chest. A few seconds later I hear someone say, *boy!* Then a little cry. Nurse yells, *48!* A few more seconds I hear a little cry.

Daddy: *That's it?*

Aiden: Big yell and crying *Waaaaaaaaaaaaah!*

Daddy: *Hey Man! Heeeeey! Oh my God! Look at him looking like me! Look baby* (as they drape him over the partition) *look at your little guy. All that hair! Where you going with all that hair?!* (laughing)

Me: Crying. *Yaaaaaay!!*

Daddy: while at changing table *Hey Aiden! What happened? What they do?*

Aiden: Crying while getting cleaned.

Daddy: *Yea, I'm here.*

Nurse: *All that hair!*

Daddy: *I told you, you were going to have daddy's hair.*
Note: This is definitely fake news. I prayed for his curls to me like mine and my family, my dad has really curly hair, and I know Jesus didn't fail me!

Nurse: *Opps! Over achiever already.*

Daddy: *He's an over achiever? What he do?*

Nurse: *First poop!*

Daddy: *That's a good thing?*

Nurse 2: *Yes! That's one less you have to clean up!*

Nurse: *It just shows us that everything is working properly.*

Thankfully my Husband recorded all of that because I was in euphoria laying there so relaxed like I just had a massage. I felt no discomfort or pain, just pure relaxation. A completely different experience from my fibroid removal. When they laid Aiden in my arms, he was sleeping peacefully. I couldn't stop staring at him. I look at my Husband and say *"We did it"* then I broke into tears.

While the nurses were wheeling me into the recovery room, I told them how I was dropped before. They were really upset that happened to me and ready to report it, I let them know it was at a different hospital a few years prior. The nurses were very petite, I was 280 pounds when I got to the hospital. I know I hadn't lost that much fluid and weight for them to pick me up, so I asked if they had a male nurse to help them pick me up. They affirmed they could handle it with this balloon contraption they will inflate under me, which will transfer me to the bed like an Angel. I'm side eyeing them wondering if they were on the medication I was on because I didn't know of any balloons that can transfer someone to a bed. 1+1 =2 and they were basically telling me it was 13! They laugh and promise me I'd be Ok. I brace myself for impact and before I knew it 1+1 really was 13 because I floated onto the bed like a feather!

Made me think of all the times I side-eyed or questioned God along the journey, only for Him to send His Angels to carry me through every storm with a safe landing. Once we got settled in the room I check my phone to see all the birthday wishes on social media. Hubby shared an encrypted message for me on Facebook while I was in the operating room.

> HAPPY BIRTHDAY
>
> Queen Porshea Wilkins-Agomo I have been blessed with another year to celebrate the woman, wife, mother, sister, friend, daughter, aunt and Kingdom Ambassador you continue to be and the countless lives you touch. This is your day and I'm so proud of how you continue to handle all of life's challenges, trials, tribulations, celebrations, false starts, setbacks, lessons and blessings. You've embraced them all with wisdom, grace and courage. I am inspired by you daily, the fight you have for the one's you love, your prayer life, giving heart and the gift of goodbye that you so freely give. This is a very special birthday for you, and for so many reasons. So, enjoy it because God will never go back on his promise it will surely be delivered!

It was definitely delivered! Here's what I posted along with the announcement photo idea I got from Instagram.

PROMISE KEPT
While today is my birthday there's someone else who decided it would be theirs too! Please join us in wishing our Son a Happy Birthday!
AIDEN NKWACHI WILKINS-AGOMO
(Nkwachi is Ibo for God's Promise)

Born: 7/30/2020 1:48p 7lbs 7oz 20 inches

Can't wait to share the full testimony with all of you! Nothing short of a miracle!

It was an awesome day filled with cuddles with my little stinka man! The incision from my C-section was sore, but surprisingly not painful at all. It was nothing like I experienced from my myomectomy! Cutting to remove the fibroids, plus the cut through my abdomen created layers of pain, the C-section was just the abdomen cut. I remember saying I could easily do that again, minus the getting pregnant, constipation, poor sleep and weight gain!

Everything was roses and hallmark cards for us until it was time for them to do Aiden's circumcision. Nnamdi and I wept like somebody died. The thought of Aiden being cut and in any kind of pain was unbearable for us. He just got here! We disturbed his peaceful home in my womb, brought him into a cold hospital with all these random people touching him that didn't smell like Mommy. I knew it was traumatic for him! I just wanted to hold him, keep everyone away and go home! He comes back from the procedure sleeping peacefully. I take him in my arms and hold him close for countless hours. He was released to go, but we had to track my doctor down to release me as well. Soon as she did, we packed up and got out of there. No more poking on my baby boy. He could relax at home with Mommy, Daddy and Granny (my mother) who was desperately waiting to meet her grandson.

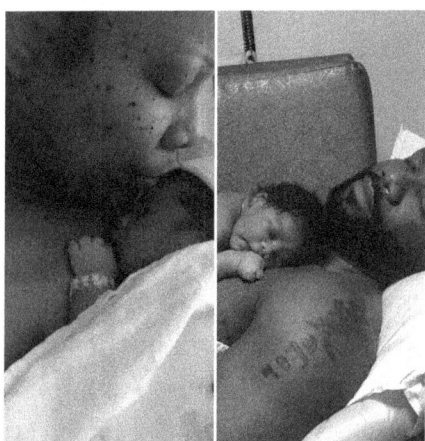

Chapter 10

EAR PLUGS

My goal was to keep Aiden safe and alive. I wasn't at peace unless he was close to me so we co-slept. I held him every night. He'd wake up to bottle feed up to four times a night. I attempted to nurse, but couldn't produce enough milk for him to stay latched, he wanted a heavy flow, so the bottle it was. I was sad about it at first because I really wanted to nurse for the experience, but I knew we'd connect just as great regardless.

I loved all the messages of support. What I didn't love was how so many people came out of nowhere with their - *if you don't do it this way, you're doing it wrong* - negative opinions. From how much I held him, to how he was fed, or where he slept; there were too many people bombarding me with their self-perceived expert advice on what they thought I needed to do. It was horrible! God created us to create. Nurturing women instinctively know how to nurture. I had to directly let them all know, thanks, but no thanks.

Bombarding a new mommy with your superstitions, rules and judgment doesn't help her at all, in fact it makes her question her ability. She's so busy thinking about what she should do and if it's right or wrong, she misses the opportunity of just being in the moment allowing things to flow naturally with her new baby. If you're going to be a support system, then support by asking her what she needs, otherwise just be quiet. I remember seeing a post on Instagram that completely summed up how I felt especially as it relates to how much I held him. It talked about how the first 90 days of a baby's life is like a 4th trimester. They are new to the world. It's cold, scary and they can't see or talk. All they know is Mommy's smell and warmth. Babies literally have anxiety attacks when left alone. They need to be held. Everyone is in rush to get them to be independent, and they can't even hold their own head up. It's impossible to spoil a baby, it's called love and there's never too much you could give. It doesn't cripple them, it strengthens them because they know you'll be there.

Was I exhausted? Absolutely! I barely slept! Not because of how he slept, but because I couldn't stop staring at him and praying for him. I'm grateful I run my business from home, so I could catch up on my sleep during the day and take in every moment of his life without worrying about my maternity leave expiring. I stopped working the moment I found out I was pregnant and rested. I only worked when I felt like it. I didn't want to miss a second of his life. I kept him wrapped on me and slept when he did. I was told the days are long, but the years are short and I knew it would feel like only an instant of time has passed when he's grown and I'm at his wedding giving his new bride a cold stare down like she stole something! I cuddled, kissed and loved on him daily. We'd try to lay him down alone to sleep, but he wasn't having it, he needed and wanted to be held. Eventually he'd lay in his co-sleeping bed between my husband and I at night. He'd lay there and sleep after his feedings. I still kept an eye on him though, I couldn't stop marveling at how miraculous God is.

I was committed to co-sleeping with him until he was ready to be on his own which I felt would happen naturally before he turned one. My Husband was great with Aiden during the day. Every now and then at night he'd visit Mars though. Aiden couldn't sleep on his back - like all the super experts in the world says babies should. He only could sleep without choking from colic if he was on his stomach. By his second month he had enough strength to move his head side to side. He had to use momentum to do it, but my little super baby made it happen, he was scooting by eight weeks old! Anytime he'd have an episode of coughing or spitting up we used an electronic aspirator to help clear his throat and nose out.

One night Aiden was having an episode and it wasn't clearing as quickly as usual. I asked my beloved Husband to turn on the light. I continued working on Aiden thinking he heard me, and I noticed there was no movement in the bed. I yelled, *Honey!* And when I turned to look at him, while also still trying to work on Aiden, I noticed something yellow on his ear.

As I looked closer, I saw it was ear plugs! I yelled *Nnamdi! Are you wearing ear plugs?!*

He takes them out and says *"Huh?"*

Me: Completely shook. *Why are you sleeping with ear plugs and we have a newborn?!?*

Husband: *I couldn't sleep. He makes too much noise.*

Me: Blood pressure is boiling. Thinking about how much noise he makes when snoring that was uncomfortable for me and Aiden at times. Wishing Aiden was a baseball bat instead of a baby so I could get in one good swing to knock some sense into his head. I yell, *"He was choking again!"*

Husband: Jumps up half sleep like he's really about to take action.

Me: Gives him the look of sheer death.

I never saw the ear plugs again. We laugh about it now, but that night will definitely go on record as one of the crazy ones! While Aiden was living his best baby life, I went through a lot of emotions. I felt alone a lot. So much attention on the baby, but none on me. My support system wasn't supporting me like I thought they would. They assumed I didn't need anything because I'm strong and figured I'd say something if I did. The thing is, this was new to me. I didn't know what to say or ask for. They all had multiple babies so I trusted they would automatically come to me to help. They didn't. They treated me like I was normal and didn't just give birth. Expecting me to cook and do all the things for them like I was before getting pregnant. They even had the nerve to get mad because I wasn't cooking! Even though no one thought to cook anything for me.

I just made a whole human, was cut open twice to get him here, went through all kids of warfare and somehow, I'm the bad guy because I'm not catering to others while I heal. I was even compared to single mothers, and told I should figure out what to do without any help. I had a whole husband, there was no reason for me to think of anything single. That wasn't my life, and I wasn't going to start acting like it was. Then I reached my tipping point, my Husband saw I was pushed too far and called my support team to tell him how they all, he included, have dropped the ball on being there for me during this transition.

It made me wonder if they really cared like they claim they did. What hidden emotions were they holding onto and using my moment of weakness to project their bottled-up hate? It was disappointing and hurtful. Definitely a mix of unmet and misguided expectations. An unmet expectation is when someone says they will do something and they don't. A misguided expectation is when you assume someone will do something and they don't. I quickly began to miss the peacefulness of my pregnancy and realized I probably should've prayed for a peaceful postpartum just as hard. Lesson learned! Things got better over time. The days and nights got easier. I bonded with my baby boy so beautifully. He knows above all I'm his safe place. He loves his family, but there's no match for his Supernatural Mama! I've been there every step, sacrificed sleep and whatever else, it's a love like none other. His future wife (side eye) will thank me.

Best Year Ever

Aiden's first year was so fun. Lots of time with family and crawling around after his big sister who took her role very seriously by loading his cheeks up with kisses all day. I put him in baby gymnastics at nine months old and he took over like a pro. His legs were strong from jumping in his bouncer like you all saw at the end of my Docuseries, so he began walking at ten months. We home school at the Wilkins Montessori Leadership Academy Kingdom Business Institute of Global Education (the name - jokingly - varies everyday, just know he's getting a good mix of everything!) His weekly trip to gymnastics is his time to play with other kids. He always walks to the middle of the circle where the instructor is and starts babbling and pointing, his way of telling everyone what to do. He's a natural leader and makes his rounds to interact with the other parents and kids, basically welcoming them to his gymnastic class.

One day the unthinkable happened. While in the waiting area he saw one little girl he'd always play with; I'm thinking he'll do his normal babbly hello, when this little guy leaned in and kissed her on the lips! Twice! I was shook! There were other girls there, but his heart was for Piper and apparently hers for Aiden because she let him do it! They even walked into class together afterwards. I was in my feelings big time! I saw a video once online that talked about the heartbreak boy moms experience over time. As their little guy grows and becomes more independent and confident it feels like he's breaking up with you little by little each day. Lord help me not be the annoying mother that interferes with her adult son's life, in Jesus's name, Amen!

I share more of his first year and candid moments in my blog on StraightTalkWomanTalk.com/blog including a video of him saying his ABC's and counting to ten at 15 months! You'll have plenty to share of your own as well. These little humans are forever entertaining. I can't wait to read your story! The journey to the promise will test you in every area, but no matter how much things change around you, what matters is you staying in faith, allowing God to do His work through you. My family and village wasn't restored to the former, it was rebuilt to the better. We all still have our flaws and moments of shortcomings coming out, but that just increases the flavor of our blend. When I see Aiden's face I can honestly say I'd do it all again. God is faithful.

#AidenNkwachi #GodsPromise
9 months

Chapter 11

THE STRATEGY

Now that you see what's possible, let's shift gears to strategize. There are a few definitions for strategy, the two that work for our goal are:

1. The science and art of military command exercised to meet the enemy in combat under advantageous conditions.
2. An adaptation or complex of adaptations (as of behavior, metabolism, or structure) that serves or appears to serve an important function in achieving evolutionary success.

This is relevant for a few reasons:

1. We're going to war against the devil in the spirit realm. We can't see or touch him personally, but he is there.
    - Ephesians 6:12 - For our struggle is not against flesh and blood [contending only with physical opponents], but against the rulers, against the powers, against the world forces of this [present]

- darkness, against the spiritual forces of wickedness in the heavenly (supernatural) places.
  - 1 Peter 5:8 – Be sober [well balanced and self-disciplined], be alert and cautious at all times. That enemy of yours, the devil, prowls around like a roaring lion [fiercely hungry], seeking someone to devour.

Because he is a spirit, he has to use people in the natural both knowingly and unknowingly to them, to do his work. He does this by exploiting our weaknesses; roaming around looking for areas of ignorance about him, and keeping us as far away from the Word of God as possible. He doesn't look like the image displayed in movies, you won't see a red tail or horns on someone's head. You will see a normal looking person; he is the master of manipulation, that's why the bible says to *test the spirits (1 John 4:1-6)*.

Everyone that enters your life isn't a blessing. I'm sure you've had experiences where you first met someone and they're incredible, then out of nowhere they become a completely different person in a negative way. The thing is, it was always there, just in disguise. Calculated by the enemy through the weaknesses and lack of knowledge of that individual. If the same thing keeps happening to you by different people, there is a spirit connected to them, you are attracting. When the enemy can't gain access to you directly, he uses other people in hopes you'll let your guard down. If the same thing keeps happening to you and there isn't another person involved, then he has gained access to you directly.

> Father, please reveal to me where I've given the enemy access directly or indirectly so I can eliminate it.

An enemy is anyone who tries to silence your voice or sabotage your influence. Their goal is to destroy, delay, distract and deny you from having the joy, peace, success and happiness you desire. Not having an understanding of who the fight is really against will cause you to fight the wrong battles. This leads to frustration and exhaustion like a boxer, standing in the ring, all alone, blindfolded, swinging their fists at the air. Ignorance will also cause you to fight the wrong person, this is very common in emotionally high circumstances. The devil knows our weaknesses and will exploit them to his advantage by making suggestions that cause us to think or act negatively. For example:

- You think: *My husband hasn't tried to have sex with me this week. Every time we do have sex, I'm the one initiating and I don't enjoy it.*
- The enemy whispers: *He's cheating and wants a divorce.*
- You think: *I knew it! All that time he spends on his phone isn't just for work. He's talking to another woman.*
- The enemy whispers: *Yep. Be smart girl. You deserve better. What about your Ex?*

Now you've gone down memory lane, creating an entire X-rated movie about a man who you have no business thinking about. The relationship ended because he cheated, lied, was lazy, abusive or whatever valid reason you decided on a decade ago. However; because the enemy is in your ear, in that moment you think your Ex is way better than your husband.

The truth is, your husband is constipated and just isn't in the mood. He sees you in the hallway and says hi and you ignore him. Now you're the boxer swinging at air.

So how do you fight something you can't see?

As I shared in my testimony, you do so by governing. You take authority, rule and control over your thoughts, words, actions and environment. It's an intentional process that requires your full attention and submersion.

Philippians 4:8 - Finally, believers, whatever is true, whatever is honorable and worthy of respect, whatever is right and confirmed by God's word, whatever is pure and wholesome, whatever is lovely and brings peace, whatever is admirable and of good repute; if there is any excellence, if there is anything worthy of praise, think continually on these things [center your mind on them, and implant them in your heart].

Using the example and scripture above let's see governing in action.

- He hasn't tried to have sex with you. True.
- You're the one initiating. True.
- You don't enjoy it. True.

Your feelings are valid and there's nothing wrong with that. It's the facts of the current circumstances. It's also naturally negative, you did it on your own without any help from the enemy. You're being human, but because the enemy is roaming like a lion seeking whom he may devour, he picked up on your negative thoughts and pounced. When he pounces, if you act on those negative thoughts, he wins. In order for you to win, you must counter those negative thoughts by governing. The truth is:

Your husband, who does visits Mars sometimes, loves you. He is in a completely different space mentally, with no clue whatsoever that you are thinking and feeling anything negative at all. As far as he's concerned, everything is perfect and he's the biggest, best, most romantic, hot, sexy, knight in shining armor you've ever laid eyes on, who leaves you satisfied in bed and begging for more. His ego loves your obsession with initiating sex, and as far as he's concerned, he'd be dumb to do anything different, so he lets you do your thing.

Now that you're armed with the truth, in this example, when the enemy says he's cheating, your response is to verbally say out loud: **Cancel.**

If the enemy whispers it again or you feel the pull to stay negative, stop and say again: **Cancel.**

Sometimes the negative thought stops there. If not:

1. Stand up
2. Raise your arms.
3. Cross them at your wrists to make an X in the air.
4. As you yell out cancel pull your arms down breaking the X. Your arms should be hanging straight by your side when done.

Breaking the X symbolizes breaking the connection to the whispers of the enemy. You are physically cutting the ties, slicing away the negative and destroying the enemy - your real opponent - versus swinging punches in the air fighting no one.

If you can't relate to the husband conflict then insert your own. Maybe your challenge is health. The doctors said they need to meet with you to discuss something important and you immediately think the worse, when it's really just a typo on your insurance, not the deadly disease you thought you had. The only thing the devil can do is make a suggestion through our thoughts.

The thought you don't cast down will take you down.

Regardless of what the issue is, the principle to overcome is the same. **Cancel. Cross. Declare.**

To seal the act, redirect your focus to the goal – your promised baby – and begin to declare pure, wholesome, lovely and peaceful things.

To effectively do this, you need to do one very important thing.

Name your baby

There is power in a name. It takes a thought and makes it a thing. Names are so important. We end our prayer with it when we say - *in the name of Jesus, Amen.*

- Luke 10:17 - The seventy returned with joy, saying, "Lord, even the demons are subject to us in Your name."
- James 2:19 - You believe that there is one God. You do well. Even the demons believe—and tremble!

By saying in Jesus's name or in the name of Jesus, we seal, confirm, cover and protect what we just spoke. It destroys the enemy, petitions the Kingdom of Heaven, activates God's Angels and stirs your faith.

If you have your baby's name, use it in the declarations below. If you don't yet, take a moment to think of it so you can use it.

- My husband and I have a loving and passionate relationship.
- He pursues me daily; I feel adored and satisfied when we make love.
- Every visit to the doctor is positive and I am healthy.
- I'm so happy and grateful now that I am pregnant with our baby _____ (insert baby's name).

Could you see it and feel it? Your healthy marriage? Your beautiful baby? Repetition is your weapon. The more you say it the more room you have in your mind for what's positive. By saying it out loud you can't hear the negative whisper from the enemy.

You must speak what you saw until you see what you said.

Let's say that again, but as a declarative.

I am speaking what I saw in the spirit, until I see what I said in the natural.

I am. Two very powerful words representing God Himself.

- Exodus 3:14 - God said to Moses, "I Am Who I Am"; and He said, "You shall say this to the Israelites, 'I Am has sent me to you.'"
- John 14:6 - Jesus said to him, "I am the [only] Way [to God] and the [real] Truth and the [real] Life; no one comes to the Father but through Me."
- Revelation 21:6 - And He said to me, "It is done. I am the Alpha and the Omega, the Beginning and the End. To the one who thirsts I will give [water] from the fountain of the water of life without cost.

- John 8:58 - Jesus replied, "I assure you and most solemnly say to you, before Abraham was born, I Am."

Those are just a few examples of the power in the two words I AM. God used them to represent who He is. We are made in His image and likeness (**Genesis 1:27**). He is in us. When we talk like He talks and acts like He does, we are activating our faith and putting pressure on His word. This causes Him to come down from Heaven and sit in our situation.

When He sits, we feel clarity.

When we feel clear, we create.

When we create, we change our environment.

When we change our environment, we have peace.

When we have peace, we make promise babies!

Let's tap into some I AM's. We'll do seven for completion.

I AM healed!
I AM pregnant!
I AM at peace!
I AM loved!
I AM protected!
I AM a happy wife!
I AM thankful!

Don't stop here. Make a list and personalize it for what you're believing God for.

I AM _____

I AM _____
I AM _____
I AM _____
I AM _____
I AM _____
I AM _____
I AM _____
I AM _____
I AM _____
I AM _____
I AM _____
I AM _____
I AM _____
I AM _____
I AM _____
I AM _____
I AM _____
I AM _____
I AM _____
I AM _____
I AM _____

Repetition is your best advocate. **So, then faith comes by hearing, and hearing by the word of God. (Romans 10:17)**. It activates our faith when we hear the same thing over and over. Each time something is said we grow, so the next time you hear it, it's from a different place and you receive differently.

Strategy is simple. In business I was taught that rich and wealthy people become so by doing the boring and mundane things that those who aren't rich don't want to do. There's so much truth to this. Warfare isn't always big, loud and difficult. It gets loud at the climax, yet 90% of the time things are just a consistent block of quiet and strategic actions. Repeating the same steps over and over. **Little foxes spoil big vineyards (Song of Solomon 2:15)** by consistently showing up. At times it will feel boring, you may even feel stupid yelling cancel and making an X with your arms. You may think it's not working or a waste of time. I'm here to tell you, it works.

Small hinges swing big doors.

Small letters create best-selling books.

Small sperm and egg create world changing humans.

Small keys unlock large vaults with billions of dollars.

There is so much power in small, simple and consistent.

Just like a name. I know some of you are hesitant to name your baby. You have doubt, uncertainty and fear and you think not naming it will protect you from the pain of the process. That's a lie from the enemy to keep you from activating your faith. For those of you who have already named your baby, say the prayer of encouragement below for your supernatural sister who is struggling with believing enough to name her baby.

> "Father in the name of Jesus, you are great and greatly to be praised there is none like you. You have removed the fear and activated my faith for my baby _____ (insert baby's name). Your word says in John 14:14 that if we ask you anything, presenting all that you are, in your name, you will do it. So, I ask you now, in the name of Jesus, to remove all fear, doubt and uncertainty for my supernatural sister. Replace her worry with worship, fear with faith and doubt with determination. Give her the name of her baby and the courage to speak it. In Jesus's name, Amen."

We're in this together. I understand the block. Sometimes you can't pray. It hurts so much you don't even have words. The beautiful part about God is He's omniscient, meaning all knowing. He knows what we can't do, and will always make sure we get what we need when we need it. Jehovah Jireh, our provider!

Let's recap the strategy.

1. Name your baby or babies for those of you who desire multiples, and talk to them daily.
2. Cancel the negative thought of the thing you don't want, both verbally and physically.
3. Activate your faith by declaring what you do want with I AM statements.

Simple and more than enough to defeat the enemy and inner-me standing in the way.

Common Causes of Infertility

I shared earlier that our lack of knowledge is the enemy's playground. I didn't know fibroids existed much less affect fertility, had I known I would've talked to my doctor about it. You may not know what's blocking you, so I've complied a list of some common causes of infertility to help you have the conversation with a medical professional.

1. A tumor or cyst: Tumors and cysts are two distinct entities.
    - Cyst. A cyst is a sac that may be filled with air, fluid or other material. A cyst can form in any part of

the body, including bones, organs and soft tissues. Most cysts are noncancerous (benign), but sometimes cancer can cause a cyst.
- Tumor. A tumor is any abnormal mass of tissue or swelling. Like a cyst, a tumor can form in any part of the body. A tumor can be benign or cancerous (malignant).

Cysts that appear uniform after examination by ultrasound or a computerized tomography (CT) scan are almost always benign and should simply be observed.

If the cyst has solid components, it may be benign or malignant and should have further evaluation. Often this is done with repeat imaging to see if the cyst grows over time. The best test to determine whether a cyst or tumor is benign or malignant is a biopsy. This procedure involves removing a sample of the affected tissue — or, in some cases, the entire suspicious area — and studying it under a microscope.

2. Eating disorder such as anorexia or bulimia: eating disorders are behavioral conditions characterized by severe and persistent disturbance in eating behaviors and associated distressing thoughts and emotions. They can be very serious conditions affecting physical, psychological and social function. Types of eating disorders include anorexia nervosa, bulimia nervosa, binge eating disorder, avoidant restrictive food intake disorder, other specified feeding and eating disorder, pica and rumination disorder.

3. Excessive alcohol or drug use: Regular heavy drinking (8 or more drinks per week for women and 15 for men) can affect fertility by interrupting menstrual cycle and ovulation causing changes to ovarian function, known

as amenorrhea and anovulation, respectively changing hormone levels of testosterone, estradiol and luteinizing hormone causing hyperprolactinemia or high prolactin in the blood.

After pregnancy, many drugs can pass through breast milk and harm the baby. Miscarriage, stillbirth, small size, low birth weight, premature birth, birth defects, sudden infant death syndrome, drug dependency in the baby.

4. Thyroid gland problems: Thyroid disease is a general term for a medical condition that keeps your thyroid from making the right amount of hormones. Your thyroid typically makes hormones that keep your body functioning normally. When the thyroid makes too much thyroid hormone, your body uses energy too quickly. This is called hyperthyroidism. Using energy too quickly will do more than make you tired — it can make your heart beat faster, cause you to lose weight without trying and even make you feel nervous. On the flip-side of this, your thyroid can make too little thyroid hormone. This is called hypothyroidism. When you have too little thyroid hormone in your body, it can make you feel tired, you might gain weight and you may even be unable to tolerate cold temperatures. These two main disorders can be caused by a variety of conditions. They can also be passed down through families (inherited). Untreated thyroid conditions during pregnancy are linked to serious problems, including premature birth, miscarriage and stillbirth. If your thyroid condition is treated during pregnancy, you can have a healthy pregnancy and a healthy baby.

5. Excess weight: Obesity during pregnancy puts you at risk of several serious health problems:
    - Gestational diabetes is diabetes that is first diagnosed during pregnancy. This condition can increase the risk of having a cesarean delivery.

Women who have had gestational diabetes also have a higher risk of having diabetes in the future, as do their children. Obese women are screened for gestational diabetes early in pregnancy and also may be screened later in pregnancy as well.

- Preeclampsia is a high blood pressure disorder that can occur during pregnancy or after pregnancy. It is a serious illness that affects a woman's entire body. The kidneys and liver may fail. Preeclampsia can lead to seizures, a condition called eclampsia. In rare cases, stroke can occur. Severe cases need emergency treatment to avoid these complications. The baby may need to be delivered early. Sleep apnea is a condition in which a person stops breathing for short periods during sleep.
- Sleep apnea is associated with obesity. During pregnancy, sleep apnea not only can cause fatigue but also increases the risk of high blood pressure, preeclampsia, eclampsia, and heart and lung disorders.

6. Stress: Stress is a feeling of emotional or physical tension. It can come from any event or thought that makes you feel frustrated, angry, or nervous. Stress is your body's reaction to a challenge or demand. In short bursts, stress can be positive, such as when it helps you avoid danger or meet a deadline. But when stress lasts for a long time, it may harm your health.

    A recent study found that women with high levels of alpha-amylase, an enzyme that correlates with stress, have a harder time getting pregnant.

7. Depression (major depressive disorder): Is a common and serious medical illness that negatively affects how you feel, the way you think and how you act. Fortunately, it is also treatable. Depression causes feelings of sadness and/or a loss of interest in activities you once enjoyed. It

can lead to a variety of emotional and physical problems and can decrease your ability to function at work and at home.

1. Depression symptoms can vary from mild to severe and can include:
    - Feeling sad or having a depressed mood
    - Loss of interest or pleasure in activities once enjoyed
    - Changes in appetite — weight loss or gain unrelated to dieting
    - Trouble sleeping or sleeping too much
    - Loss of energy or increased fatigue
    - Increase in purposeless physical activity (e.g., inability to sit still, pacing, handwringing) or slowed movements or speech (these actions must be severe enough to be observable by others)
    - Feeling worthless or guilty
    - Difficulty thinking, concentrating or making decisions
    - Thoughts of death or suicide
8. Anxiety Disorder: Anxiety disorders differ from normal feelings of nervousness or anxiousness, and involve excessive fear or anxiety. Anxiety refers to anticipation of a future concern and is more associated with muscle tension and avoidance behavior.

   Fear is an emotional response to an immediate threat and is more associated with a fight or flight reaction – either staying to fight or leaving to escape danger. Anxiety disorders can cause people to try to avoid situations that trigger or worsen their symptoms.
9. Problems with ovulation: Most cases of female infertility are caused by problems with ovulation. Without ovulation, there are no eggs to be fertilized. Some signs that

a woman is not ovulating normally include irregular or absent menstrual periods. Ovulation problems are often caused by polycystic ovarian syndrome (PCOS). PCOS is a hormone imbalance problem which can interfere with normal ovulation. PCOS is the most common cause of female infertility. Primary ovarian insufficiency (POI) is another cause of ovulation problems. POI occurs when a woman's ovaries stop working normally before she is 40. POI is not the same as early menopause.

10. Problems with the cervix: The cervix is the lower portion of the uterus that protrudes into the vagina. Common symptoms related to conditions of the cervix include vaginal discharge, spotting, bleeding, pain, pressure, or discomfort. Such symptoms can be caused by inflammation, infection, injury, allergy, precancerous cellular changes, or cervical cancer.

    Inflammation and allergy can be caused by chemicals, lubricants, condoms and devices that come in contact with the cervix, depending upon their composition. Many cervical infections, including chlamydia, gonorrhea, trichomoniasis, herpes, and human papilloma virus, or HPV, are transmitted through sexual contact. Changes in cervical cells can occur due to chronic inflammation or infection, and can sometimes develop into cancers.

    Depending upon the cause of cervix symptoms and their extent or severity, other symptoms may accompany cervix symptoms. In the case of infection, inflammation, and allergy, there also may be vaginal itching, swelling or odor. Advanced cervical cancers can cause symptoms such as changes in bowel or bladder function, leaking of urine or stool into the vagina, leg pain and swelling, generalized fatigue, loss of appetite, and weight loss.

    Diagnosis of the cause of cervix symptoms often requires evaluating potential exposures and medical history as well as a pelvic exam. A pelvic exam includes looking at the cervix using a speculum, taking samples, and a bimanual exam, or palpation of the uterus, tubes and ovaries. The exam generally includes testing for sexually transmitted diseases (STDs), including chlamydia, gonorrhea, HIV, syphilis and hepatitis C.

Other tests may be done depending upon the suspected cause. Treatment varies based on the condition, but many cervix symptoms resolve with appropriate treatment. Sexual partners should be notified and offered treatment for STDs.

Sometimes, cervix symptoms can accompany a serious or potentially life-threatening condition. Seek immediate medical care (call 911) for symptoms such as uncontrolled or heavy bleeding, bleeding during pregnancy, high fever (higher than 101 degrees Fahrenheit), or severe pain in the pelvis or abdomen. Cervix symptoms often require treatment to avoid complications. If you have cervix symptoms, seek prompt medical care.

11. Age: A woman is born with all the eggs she is going to have in her lifetime. Her eggs age with her, decreasing in quality and quantity. Age is the single most important factor affecting a woman's fertility. While good health improves the chance of getting pregnant and having a healthy baby, it doesn't override the effects of age on a woman's fertility.

A woman's best reproductive years are in her 20s. Fertility gradually declines in the 30s, particularly after age 35. Each month that she tries, a healthy, fertile 30-year-old woman has a 20% chance of getting pregnant. That means that for every 100 fertile 30-year-old women trying to get pregnant in 1 cycle, 20 will be successful and the other 80 will have to try again. By age 40, a woman's chance is less than 5% per cycle, so fewer than 5 out of every 100 women are expected to be successful each month.

Women do not remain fertile until menopause. The average age for menopause is 51, but most women become unable to have a successful pregnancy sometime in their mid-40s. These percentages are true for natural conception as well as conception using fertility treatment, including in vitro fertilization (IVF). Although stories in the news media may lead women and their partners to believe that they will be to able use fertility treatments such as IVF to get pregnant, a woman's age affects the success rates of infertility treatments. The age-related loss of female fertility happens because both the quality and the quantity of eggs gradually decline.

12. Damage to the fallopian tubes or uterus: It can be caused by one or more of the following:
    - Pelvic inflammatory disease: Pelvic inflammatory disease (PID) is an infection of the female reproductive organs. It most often occurs when sexually transmitted bacteria spread from your vagina to your uterus, fallopian tubes or ovaries. The signs and symptoms of pelvic inflammatory disease can be subtle or mild. Some women don't experience any signs or symptoms. As a result, you might not realize you have it until you have trouble getting pregnant or you develop chronic pelvic pain.
    - A previous infection
    - Polyps in the uterus: Polyps are abnormal tissue growths that most often look like small, flat bumps or tiny mushroom like stalks. Most polyps are small and less than half an inch wide. Polyps in the colon are the most common, but it's also possible to develop polyps in places that include: ear canal. cervix. The main difference between fibroids and

polyps is the tissue they are made of. As mentioned earlier, fibroids are made of a connective fibrous tissue, whereas polyps are made up of the same tissue that makes up the uterine lining, also known as endometrial tissue.
- Fibroids: Abnormal growths that develop in or on a woman's uterus. Sometimes these tumors become quite large and cause severe abdominal pain and heavy periods. In other cases, they cause no signs or symptoms at all. The growths are typically benign, or noncancerous. The cause of fibroids is unknown.
- Endometriosis: Is an often painful disorder in which tissue similar to the tissue that normally lines the inside of your uterus — the endometrium — grows outside your uterus. Endometriosis most commonly involves your ovaries, fallopian tubes and the tissue lining your pelvis.
- Scar tissue or adhesions: Intrauterine Adhesions, Asherman's Syndrome – Scar Tissue In Uterine Cavity - The condition of scarring within the endometrial cavity of the uterus is often referred to as Asherman's Syndrome. A normal uterine cavity and endometrial lining is necessary in order to conceive and maintain a pregnancy. Scar tissue within the uterine cavity can partially or completely obliterate the normal cavity and can interfere with conception, or increase the risk for miscarriage or other complications later in the pregnancy.
- Causes of Asherman's Syndrome: It is most commonly caused by the trauma to the lining from a D&C (dilation and curettage)

- A recently pregnant uterus is much more susceptible to developing Asherman's after D&C compared to a non-pregnant uterus.
- It is sometimes caused by scarring after uterine surgeries such as Cesarean section, myomectomy for fibroid tumors or abortion.
- In rare cases it is caused by infection, such as genital tuberculosis (rare in the US)
- We have seen some women with uterine adhesions that have never had any D&C or other surgery – some cases of Asherman's are of unknown cause

13. Chronic medical illness: Chronic diseases are defined broadly as conditions that last 1 year or more and require ongoing medical attention or limit activities of daily living or both. Chronic diseases such as heart disease, cancer, and diabetes are the leading causes of death and disability in the United States. They are also leading drivers of the nation's $3.8 trillion in annual health care costs. Many chronic diseases are caused by a short list of risk behaviors:
    - Tobacco use and exposure to secondhand smoke.
    - Poor nutrition, including diets low in fruits and vegetables and high in sodium and saturated fats.
    - Lack of physical activity.
    - Excessive alcohol use.
14. Previous ectopic (tubal) pregnancy: Ectopic pregnancy, also called extrauterine pregnancy, is when a fertilized egg grows outside a woman's uterus, somewhere else in their belly. It can cause life-threatening bleeding and needs medical care right away. In more than 90% of cases, the egg implants in a fallopian tube. This is called a tubal pregnancy.

15. Genetic conditions: Certain genetic conditions may affect fertility or may be treated through a variation of in vitro fertilization (IVF). In general, these genetic abnormalities fall into two categories: Single gene defects and chromosomal abnormalities.

    Single gene defects involve a mutation or abnormality within the DNA which codes for a particular gene. Single gene defects can lead to health conditions that can cause fertility problems. These conditions include cystic fibrosis, Tay Sachs disease, spinal muscular atrophy, Canavan disease, sickle cell disease, and Thalassemias. Chromosomal abnormalities include changes in the number or structure of the chromosomes which carry the DNA. These changes often affect many genes. The normal number of chromosomes for humans is 46. Women have 22 pairs of autosomes and two X chromosomes. Men have 22 pairs of autosomes and one X and one Y chromosome. Examples of chromosomal abnormalities include Down syndrome (Trisomy 21—an extra chromosome 21), Turner syndrome (loss of one X chromosome) and Klinefelter syndrome (an extra X chromosome in men). In men, chromosome abnormalities can be associated with low sperm counts. Y-chromosome gene deletions and cystic fibrosis gene mutations may be associated with azoospermia or a lack of sperm. Cystic fibrosis gene mutations also may result in an absence of the ducts that transport sperm. Genetic testing is recommended for all men with a lack of sperm (azoospermia) or low sperm counts. In women, chromosomal abnormalities can be associated with pregnancy loss or even clinical conditions in children such as Down syndrome.

    Diagnosis: Some genetic conditions that affect fertility occur more frequently in certain populations: Tay Sachs disease (Ashkenazi Jews and French Canadians), Canavan disease (Ashkenazi Jews), sickle cell disease (African Americans, Hispanics and Mediterraneans), and Thalassemias (Mediterranean, Middle East and East Asians). CIRS physicians may suggest genetic tests for single gene defects as part of the initial infertility evaluation, especially if either partner is from one of these ethnic groups or if a partner has a family history of certain diseases such as cystic fibrosis. A history of recurrent miscarriages also would require chromosomal testing of both partners.

16. DES syndrome: (The medication DES, given to women to prevent miscarriage or premature birth can result in fertility problems for their children.) Diethylstilbestrol syndrome (DES syndrome) refers to developmental or health problems caused by exposure to DES before birth (in utero), such as reproductive tract differences, infertility, and an increased risk for certain cancers.[1][2] DES is a synthetic form of the female hormone estrogen that was prescribed to pregnant women between about 1940 and 1971 to prevent miscarriage and premature labor. DES also may have been prescribed to women to inhibit lactation, as hormone replacement therapy for menopause symptoms, and as a post-coital emergency contraceptive ("morning-after pill").[3] It was first thought to be safe and effective, but studies later found that DES was not effective in preventing pregnancy complications, and caused health problems in some children of mothers exposed during pregnancy, as well as some of the women exposed during pregnancy or for other reasons.[1] It is important to note that not all people exposed to DES have health problems due to the exposure.

 · Females exposed to DES in utero may have reproductive tract differences affecting the uterus, fallopian tubes, cervix, and/or vagina.[1][4] Examples

include incomplete development of the uterus or cervix, a differently-shaped uterus or cervix, and a transverse vaginal septum. These differences may increase the risk of infertility.[4] Females exposed to DES in utero also are more likely to experience various pregnancy complications including ectopic pregnancy, miscarriage, and preterm birth.[1][4] However, most have healthy babies.[5] Additionally, females exposed in utero are at increased risk to develop cancers such as vaginal or cervical clear cell adenocarcinoma, squamous cervical cancer, and breast cancer.[1][3][4]
- Males exposed to DES in utero have not been studied as extensively as females, but may be at increased risk for epididymal cysts, undescended testes, and inflammation or infection of the testicles.[1][2][4] Males exposed to DES do not appear to have an increased risk of infertility.[1][3][4]
- Of note, women exposed to DES after birth (those exposed while they were pregnant or those exposed for other reasons) have an increased risk of developing breast cancer.[3][4] The children of women exposed to DES in utero (grandchildren of mothers exposed during pregnancy) may also have an increased risk for cancer, as well as higher infertility rates.[3]
- Treatment for health problems associated with DES exposure depends on each person's signs and symptoms. Women who took DES during pregnancy or for other reasons are encouraged to inform their doctors and children of the exposure, and children exposed in utero should inform their doctors so they can be monitored for possible health problems that may arise.[4]

- Abnormal cervical mucus can also cause female infertility. Abnormal cervical mucus can prevent the sperm from reaching the egg or make it more difficult for the sperm to penetrate the egg.
17. Hormone Imbalance: Too much or too little of a certain hormone. While some hormone levels fluctuate throughout your lifetime and may just be the result of natural aging, other changes occur when your endocrine glands (similar to the nervous system in that it plays a vital role in controlling and regulating many of the body's functions) get of track.

That's a lot, I know. As I shared in my story, when I found out I had fibroids, I immediately thought it was sexually transmitted. After getting more information I learned they weren't sexually transmitted and there is no real cause of them. Would've been great to know something about them beforehand so I wouldn't have stressed myself sick.

If you've found your setback on the list above, congratulations. You know more about it and now can proceed with wisdom for warfare. If you think or have been told you're infertile, the list of common causes above can help you have a better conversation with your doctor. Asking the right questions can help them look deeper into something that they may not have considered before.

Chapter 12

THE SUPERNATURAL

The word supernatural is a portmanteau, a blend or combination of words to make one. It's the combination of the super (God) and the natural (you and your doctor) that make the miracles happen. Supernatural means departing from what is usual or normal especially so as to appear to transcend the laws of nature. I like the last part: transcend (to rise above or go beyond the limits of) the laws of nature. Exceedingly above just like in **Ephesians 3:20**. God isn't like nature, He is the creator of nature. Nature and all things natural are subject and must answer to Him. There is a big difference. While natural law exists, by yielding to Him we're able to tap into a law greater and more superior than all others called, miracles. I don't know where you are in your fertility journey but one thing I do know is, God is there as well.

"This is the [remarkable degree of] confidence which we [as believers are entitled to] have before Him: that if we ask anything according to His will, [that is, consistent with His plan and purpose] He hears us." 1 John 5:14.

Below is a collection of scriptures along with declarations I recommend you say daily, in addition to what the Holy Spirit guides you to do.

SCRIPTURES AND DECLARATIONS FOR HEALING, FAITH ACTIVATION AND PEACE WITH THE PROCESS

- Luke 13:13: Then He laid His hands on her; and immediately she stood erect again and she began glorifying and praising God.

    Declaration: (lay hands on your womb) Father rest your hands on me, your healing hands. I know you are with me now, so as you do, I will stand strong and bold for you. I will shout and glorify your name for you are good and deserve all praise. I receive my healing. In Jesus's name, Amen. (Begin to praise and thank Him)

- Luke 6:15-19: Then Jesus came down with them and stood on a level place; and there was a large crowd of His disciples, and a vast multitude of people from all over Judea and Jerusalem and the coastal region of Tyre and Sidon, who had come to listen to Him and to be healed of their diseases. Even those who were troubled by unclean spirits (demons) were being healed. All the people were trying to touch Him, because [healing] power was coming from Him and healing them all.

    Declaration: Jesus I know you hold the power to heal.

I come to you from _____ (your city) just as your disciples and the crowds from Judea and Jerusalem. My yearning for what you did for them is high. I ask, in your name for you to do for me the same. I receive my healing. In Jesus's name, Amen.

- Matthew 17:20 - He answered, "Because of your little faith [your lack of trust and confidence in the power of God]; for I assure you and most solemnly say to you, if you have [living] faith the size of a mustard seed, you will say to this mountain, 'Move from here to there,' and [if it is God's will] it will move; and nothing will be impossible for you.

Declaration: Lord my faith is wavering. Sometimes its hard to believe. I know you're just and fair. I know you care. Even though I have uncertainty I will lean on your Word and take the little faith I do have and sow it into you. Mountain of _____ (insert diagnosis) move from me now, and never return again. I receive my healing. In Jesus's name, Amen.

- Luke 13:11-12 - And there was a woman who for eighteen years had had an illness caused by a spirit (demon). She was bent double, and could not straighten up at all. When Jesus saw her, He called her over and said to her, "Woman, you are released from your illness."

Declaration: Father my ears are ringing and heart is open. I am ready to be released from my illness. It has been _____ (number of years since you've had it). Please reveal to me what I else I need to do make it go away.

I believe you will do it for me. I receive my healing. In Jesus's name, Amen.

- **Psalm 107:20-21**: He sent His word and healed them, And rescued them from their destruction. Let them give thanks to the Lord for His lovingkindness, And for His wonderful acts to the children of men!

Declaration: You sent your word and healed me, and recused me from my destruction. Lord, I thank you for your lovingkindness and for your wonderful acts to me!

Yes, now. Even while you're sick and broken. Say this. Nothing will activate your faith and fire up the Heavens like speaking those things that haven't happened, as though they already have. Angels will flock to you, even sit in your room when you do. That confidence you feel afterwards is the Holy Spirit physically lifting you up to straighten your posture. There is no chiropractor who's greater!

- **Psalm 147:3** - He heals the brokenhearted and binds up their wounds [healing their pain and comforting their sorrow].

Declaration: Lord you know the condition of my heart. The beats are painful. Thank you for holding me, listening to me and caring for me. I receive my healing. In Jesus's name, Amen.

Loss is a heavy burden to carry. Many of you have suffered tremendous loss along your fertility journey. From failed IVF cycles, to miscarriages, to stillborn, the emotional weight on your heart is unbearable. Can I share something with you? Even though the pain and disappointment make you feel alone, you're not. You're actually closer to God than ever before. There's nothing that gets His attention more than the cry of His daughter. The wind on your face, butterfly on your shoulder, chill up your spine, goosebumps on your arms are all hugs from The Father. Subtle and simple reminders letting you know He hears and is nearby.

- Psalm 103:2-3 - Bless and affectionately praise the Lord, O my soul, And do not forget any of His benefits; Who forgives all your sins, Who heals all your diseases.

Declaration: Father please forgive me for all my sins. Forgive me for _____ (name them). I repent of it all. I want to be made new and whole in you. I want to honor your likeness that is in me. I loose, bind and cast out any and every connection to _____ (name of person you believe you contracted it from). I receive my healing. In Jesus's name, Amen.

STD's are horrible. Whether the consensual (agreed upon) sex was protected or not, you participated. You didn't know he had an STD, and didn't care to ask, or maybe you did and he lied, but now you have it too. Some are curable, others are not and only treatable. Never did you think that fun night in your 20's would show up to haunt you in your 30's and 40's, especially when you've decided to settle down. It happens a lot so don't think you're the only one, and please don't walk around in shame. You're not less worthy to be a mother.

You've accepted responsibility by admitting to God you were wrong, and have earned His forgiveness by simply asking Him to do so. Now, you need to do the hard thing and forgive yourself. Focus on what you can and need to do moving forward to ensure that STD doesn't affect your health and ability to conceive. That's the work.

- Mark 5:34 - Then He said to her, "Daughter, your faith [your personal trust and confidence in Me] has restored you to health; go in peace and be [permanently] healed from your suffering."

Declaration: My faith is high and my health is restored. I am at peace and no longer suffering.

- Luke 8:47-48 - When the woman saw that she had not escaped notice, she came up trembling and fell down before Him. She declared in the presence of all the people the reason why she had touched Him, and how she had been immediately healed. 48 He said to her, "Daughter, your faith [your personal trust and confidence in Me] has made you well. Go in peace (untroubled, undisturbed well-being)."

Declaration: Father I touch you just as she did. I trust and am confident I am healed just as she was.

- Jeremiah 33:6 - Behold, [in the restored Jerusalem] I will bring to it health and healing, and I will heal them; and I will reveal to them an abundance of peace (prosperity, security, stability) and truth.

Declaration: In _____ (your last name) home there is health, healing, an abundance of peace and truth. We receive it all, in the name of Jesus.

While you can't change the facts of our diagnosis, you can change your perspective of it by focusing on the truth - God can heal, and what's most encouraging He will. A great way to activate your faith is by making this scripture personal.

- Psalm 113:9 - He makes the barren (infertile) woman live in the house a joyful mother of children. Praise the Lord! (Hallelujah!)

Declaration: He makes me _____ (your full name) the barren woman who lives in _____ (your address) a joyful mother of children. I receive my child(ren)_____ (the name(s) of your unborn child(ren) in Jesus's name.

What a word! Praise Him and personalize it.

- Genesis 16:11 - The Angel of the Lord continued, "Behold, you are with child, And you will bear a son; And you shall name him Ishmael (God hears), Because the Lord has heard and paid attention to your persecution (suffering).

Declaration: I am with child. I will bear a _____ (son/daughter) I will name him/her _____ because God, you heard me and have paid attention to my suffering. I receive my baby(ies) in Jesus's name.

God wants us to believe now and anyway. Name your child and begin talking to him/her now as you will when they are in your arms. For years when Jarrod and I would talk about how life will be when Aiden arrives, we'd act it out. One of his favorite things to do would be to grab a bottle of water or pillow and sit it in his lap supported by his left arm and talk to it AS IF it were Aiden and say *hey man! Come watch the game with Daddy.* He did it more and more after we got pregnant. We'd even make space between us on the couch where Aiden would sit with his bottle watching a movie with us. Sometimes he'd pass him to me and say, h*ere go to your Mommy.* Yes, all this with a water bottle or pillow. 5 years later I have a collection of photos where the water bottle is on the table, pillow by his side, and his beloved Son is in his lap. I don't care how crazy you look or how long it takes - do whatever you need to do to feel your dream. The moment you do it the closer you get to living it. Day dreaming can be real life if you just picture it first.

- Luke 1:44-45 - For behold, when the sound of your greeting reached my ears, the baby in my womb leaped for joy. And blessed [spiritually fortunate and favored by God] is she who believed and confidently trusted that there would be a fulfillment of the things that were spoken to her [by the angel sent] from the Lord."

Declaration: My baby is leaping in Heaven. I can feel them in my heart. I am blessed, because I believe and confidently trust that there will be a fulfillment of the things that were spoken to me from the Lord. I receive my promised child(ren), in Jesus's name.

- Genesis 25:21 - Isaac prayed to the Lord for his wife, because she was unable to conceive children; and the Lord granted his prayer and Rebekah his wife conceived [twins].

    Declaration: Lord thank you for a husband who prays for me! Thank you for pulling on his heart and turning it towards me to support and cover me naturally. I receive my blessing, in Jesus's name.

    Even if your husband isn't praying for you or as much as you pray, continue to affirm he is. Trying to force him will only frustrate you. Your fight isn't alone, but it is yours so you'll have to lead a lot and many times on your own. It's ok. It doesn't mean your husband doesn't care, or that he doesn't want the baby as much as you. God has him on a journey too. Just continue to speak and affirm how you'd like him to be, trusting Gods' will to be done.

- Hebrews 11:11 - By faith even Sarah herself received the ability to conceive [a child], even [when she was long] past the normal age for it, because she considered Him who had given her the promise to be reliable and true [to His word].

    Declaration: I will conceive by faith!

- Luke 1:41 - When Elizabeth heard Mary's greeting, her baby leaped in her womb; and Elizabeth was filled with the Holy Spirit and empowered by Him.

Declaration: Lord surround me with your daughters who make my purpose baby leap in my womb. Women who encourage me, uplift me, support me and stay by my side. I receive my blessing, in Jesus's name.

Who you have around you during this time is so critical. I only shared my journey with a chosen few. Everyone won't understand the depth you have to go to, in order to become who God needs you to become, so you can carry who He's called to lead the next generation. It is that big. It is that important. Use wisdom when sharing. Less in most cases is more, to protect your vision and dream.

- Isaiah 66:9 - "Shall I bring to the moment of birth and not give delivery?" says the Lord. "Or shall I who gives delivery shut the womb?" says your God.

Declaration: Lord I know you will deliver for me. Just as you have for the countless other daughters you have before me. I receive my promised baby(babies) in Jesus's name, Amen.

- 1 Samuel 1:27 - For this child I prayed, and the Lord has granted me my request which I asked of Him.

Declaration: For my child(ren) _____ (insert name) I pray and know the Lord will grant me my request. I receive my blessing, in Jesus's name, Amen.

- 1 Samuel 1:20 - It came about in due time, after Hannah had conceived, that she gave birth to a son;

she named him Samuel, saying, "Because I have asked for him from the Lord."

Declaration: Lord because you did it for Hannah, I believe you will do it for me. I've asked just as she. Thank you for blessing me, in Jesus's name, Amen.

- James 5:13-15 - Is anyone among you suffering? He must pray. Is anyone joyful? He is to sing praises [to God]. Is anyone among you sick? He must call for the elders (spiritual leaders) of the church and they are to pray over him, anointing him with oil in the name of the Lord; and the prayer of faith will restore the one who is sick, and the Lord will raise him up; and if he has committed sins, he will be forgiven.

Declaration: (grab your anointed oil) As I lay hands on myself I decree and declare healing, restoration, faith activation and peace over my life, my marriage, my womb, my career, my house and all things that concern me. Lord I thank you.

When things are bad, pray and praise. When things are good, pray and praise. When it's lonely, seek help. The church is everywhere, because it's in people. For many of you this book is your church. It is where you've come for healing and support. So don't take that part of the scripture so literal that you don't seek or allow someone to help you. It could very well come from a random person in the grocery store, you never know, so be open.

Ask God to open your spiritual eyes so you can see Him

in them. When you invite Him in, the Holy Spirit will be your guide. Coincidences are what I like to call Kingdom confirmations. Unexplainable encounters that give you exactly what you needed to get to the next step in your faith walk.

- Deuteronomy 7:13 - He will love you and bless you and multiply you; He will also bless the fruit of your womb and the fruit of your land, your grain and your new wine and your [olive] oil, the offspring of your cattle and the young of your flock, in the land which He swore to your fathers to give you.

Declaration: God, you love me, bless me and will multiply me. You have already blessed the fruit of my womb and the fruit of my land, my grain and my new wine, my oil, the offspring of my cattle and the young of my flock in the land which you swore to my fathers to give me. I receive my blessings, In Jesus's name, Amen.

- Luke 1:14 - You will have great joy and delight, and many will rejoice over his birth.

Declaration: I will have great joy and delight and many will rejoice over the birth of my son/daughter(s)_____ insert name. In Jesus's name, Amen.

- Judges 13:3 - And the Angel of the Lord appeared to the woman and said to her, "Behold, you are infertile and have no children, but you shall conceive and give birth to a son.

Declaration: The Angel of the Lord will appear to me and tell me I shall conceive and give birth to my baby. I receive my promised child(ren) in Jesus's name, Amen.

- 1 Samuel 2:21 - And [the time came when] the Lord visited Hannah, so that she conceived and gave birth to three sons and two daughters. And the boy Samuel grew before the Lord.

Declaration: Hannah conceived and so will I. I receive it in Jesus's name.

- Proverbs 31:28 - Her children rise up and call her blessed (happy, prosperous, to be admired); Her husband also, and he praises her, saying, "Many daughters have done nobly, and well [with the strength of character that is steadfast in goodness], But you excel them all."

Declaration: My children rise up and call me blessed, and my husband praises my strength and character. In Jesus's name, Amen.

- Genesis 21:1-2 - The Lord graciously remembered and visited Sarah as He had said, and the Lord did for her as He had promised. So Sarah conceived and gave birth to a son for Abraham in his old age, at the appointed time of which God had spoken to him.

Declaration: Just like Sarah I will give birth. My age is

irrelevant. My God will subtract the clock and reserve time for me. He will do it. I believe. In Jesus's name, Amen.

- Luke 1:36-37 - And listen, even your relative Elizabeth has also conceived a son in her old age; and she who was called barren is now in her sixth month. For with God nothing [is or ever] shall be impossible."

Declaration: I know women who have conceived past what society considers old age. I'm not concerned about their clock. The God I serve is the author of time and He is on my side. I'm no longer barren, my baby is ready in Heaven. I am with child, in Jesus's name, Amen.

- Exodus 23:26 - No one shall suffer miscarriage or be barren in your land; I will fulfill the number of your days.

Declaration: I will not suffer miscarriage or be barren in my land. God will fulfill the number of my days. I receive it, in Jesus's name!

- Genesis 25:24 - When her days to be delivered were fulfilled, behold, there were twins in her womb.

Declaration: I decree and declare multiples _____ (insert your desired number) are in my womb, in Jesus's name.

- Matthew 1:23 - "Behold, the virgin shall be with child and give birth to a Son, and they shall call His name Immanuel"—which, when translated, means, "God with us."

Declaration: I shall be with child and give birth to a _____ (insert gender) and they shall call his/her/their name(s) _____ which mean _____. I receive it now, in Jesus's name. Amen.

- 2 Corinthians 12:8-10 - Concerning this I pleaded with the Lord three times that it might leave me; but He has said to me, "My grace is sufficient for you [My lovingkindness and My mercy are more than enough—always available—regardless of the situation]; for [My] power is being perfected [and is completed and shows itself most effectively] in [your] weakness." Therefore, I will all the more gladly boast in my weaknesses, so that the power of Christ [may completely enfold me and] may dwell in me. So I am well pleased with weaknesses, with insults, with distresses, with persecutions, and with difficulties, for the sake of Christ; for when I am weak [in human strength], then I am strong [truly able, truly powerful, truly drawing from God's strength].

Declaration: This journey has been tough, but I know Lord, when I'm weak you are with me. I thank you for caring for and covering me. I know the miracle is on the way and I'm grateful you chose me. I and my child(ren) are yours Father, have your way. In Jesus's name, Amen.

After you pray, talk to your babies. Speak to your promise. Edify the desires of your heart. Pray for them. Plead the blood of Jesus over every body part and organ you can think of. Be specific. Design your baby as you wish. A custom order for your Father to fulfill.

His hand is in everything at all times! As I was in my office editing my Supernatural Pregnancy Docuseries, God reminded me of when Pinky in South Africa wrote her prayer for me and put it in her prayer box. While watching the video I noticed two things; one, my prayer was the 3rd one she pulled out of the box, and two, the date she wrote on it was December 15, 2017. I was pregnant on the exact same day two years later and didn't know it. He is the Master Orchestrator! All we have to do is trust His time.

> *"Call to Me and I will answer you, and tell you [and even show you] great and mighty things, [things which have been confined and hidden], which you do not know and understand and cannot distinguish."* - Jeremiah 33:3

REFERENCES

https://www.mcleodhealth.org/blog/fibroids-greater-in-african-american-women-than-white-but-why/

https://www.uofmhealth.org/health-library/hw182148#:~:text=Myomectomy%20is%20the%20surgical%20removal,who%20want%20to%20become%20pregnant

https://www.healthline.com/health/hormonal-imbalance#Understanding-hormonal-imbalance

https://www.mayoclinic.org/diseases-conditions/cancer/expert-answers/tumor/faq-20057829

https://www.psychiatry.org/patients-families/eating-disorders/what-are-eating-disorders

https://www.healthline.com/health/does-alcohol-kill-sperm-2#effect-on-female-fertility

https://my.clevelandclinic.org/health/diseases/8541-thyroid-disease#:~:text=Thyroid%20disease%20is%20a%20general,This%20is%20called%20hyperthyroidism

https://www.marchofdimes.org/complications/thyroid-conditions-during-pregnancy.aspx#:~:text=The%20thyroid%20makes%20hormones%20that,premature%20birth%2C%20miscarriage%20and%20stillbirth

https://www.acog.org/womens-health/faqs/obesity-and-pregnancy#:~:text=Pregnancy%20loss%E2%80%94Obese%20women%20have,defects%20and%20neural%20tube%20defects

https://health.usnews.com/health-news/family-health/womens-health/articles/2010/08/27/cant-get-pregnant-how-stress-may-be-causing-your-infertility#:~:text=But%20as%20unwelcome%20as%20the,a%20harder%20time%20getting%20pregnant

https://www.marchofdimes.org/complications/stress-and-pregnancy.aspx#:~:text=High%20levels%20of%20stress%20that,5%20pounds%2C%208%20ounces)

https://www.psychiatry.org/patients-families/depression/what-is-depression

https://www.psychiatry.org/patients-families/anxiety-disorders/what-are-anxiety-disorders

https://www.womenshealth.gov/a-z-topics/infertility#:~:text=Ovulation%20problems%20are%20often%20caused,another%20cause%20of%20ovulation%20problems

https://www.healthgrades.com/right-care/womens-health/cervix-symptoms#:~:text=Cervix%20symptoms%20may%20be%20caused,by%20the%20bacterium%20Chlamydia%20trachomatis

https://www.betterhealth.vic.gov.au/health/ConditionsAndTreatments/age-and-fertility

https://www.reproductivefacts.org/news-and-publications/patient-fact-sheets-and-booklets/documents/fact-sheets-and-info-booklets/age-and-fertility/

https://www.usafibroidcenters.com/blog/fibroids-vs-polyps/#:~:text=The%20main%20difference%20between%20fibroids,also%20known%20as%20endometrial%20tissue

https://www.healthline.com/health/uterine-fibroids#:~:text=Fibroids%20are%20abnormal%20growths%20that,cause%20of%20fibroids%20is%20unknown

https://www.mayoclinic.org/diseases-conditions/endometriosis/symptoms-causes/syc-20354656#:~:text=Endometriosis%20(en%2Ddoe%2Dme,the%20tissue%20lining%20your%20pelvis

https://advancedfertility.com/2020/09/17/intrauterine-adhesions-ashermans-syndrome-scar-tissue-in-uterine-cavity/

https://www.webmd.com/baby/pregnancy-ectopic-pregnancy#1

https://www.brighamandwomens.org/obgyn/infertility-reproductive-surgery/genetic-conditions#:~:text=Single%20gene%20defects%20can%20lead,sickle%20cell%20disease%2C%20and%20Thalassemias

https://rarediseases.info.nih.gov/diseases/1859/diethylstilbestrol-syndrome#ref_14346

https://www.merriam-webster.com/dictionary/strategy

ABOUT

**PURPOSE MIDWIFE.
AUTHOR. ENTREPRENEUR.**

Porshea Wilkins-Agomo (born Porshea Mitchell of Hearne, Texas) is a Purpose Midwife, Author and Entrepreneur who resides in Houston, Texas with her Husband Jarrod, son Aiden and daughter Chandler.

PURPOSE MIDWIFE

In 2014, while recovering from a myomectomy to remove multiple grapefruit size fibroids from her uterus, God gave her the assignment for her ministry Straight Talk Woman Talk International. She serves as a Purpose Midwife for thousands of women globally where she leverages supernatural strategies to teach those assigned to her how to push past their pain and give birth to their purpose.

AUTHOR

Porshea is the Author of her book You're Not Infertile, You're Just Not in Timing - supernatural strategies to activate your faith in fertility. The book showcases her uncommon faith activating journey to conceive her miracle baby boy. Serving as evidence to all that when you practice God's principles you can participate in His promises.

ENTREPRENEUR

Porshea is Founder of the Virtual Business Boutique; a branding, marketing and web design agency. She also leads an organization of professionals across multiple continents in the Network Marketing profession alongside her Husband. Their vision to Build It For Your Last Name (BIFYLN) has allowed them to develop one of the most admired organizations in the profession.

EDUCATION + ACCOLADES

Porshea earned a B.B.A. in Marketing from Sam Houston State University in Huntsville, Texas, received Congressional Recognition for community development and managed the development of a $1.4 Billion brand in the retail industry.

CONNECT ON SOCIAL MEDIA

@PorsheaWilkins
ACROSS ALL PLATFORMS

FOR BOOKING & MEDIA:
PorsheaWilkins.com

Supernatural Pregnancy Docuseries

Docuseries Reviews

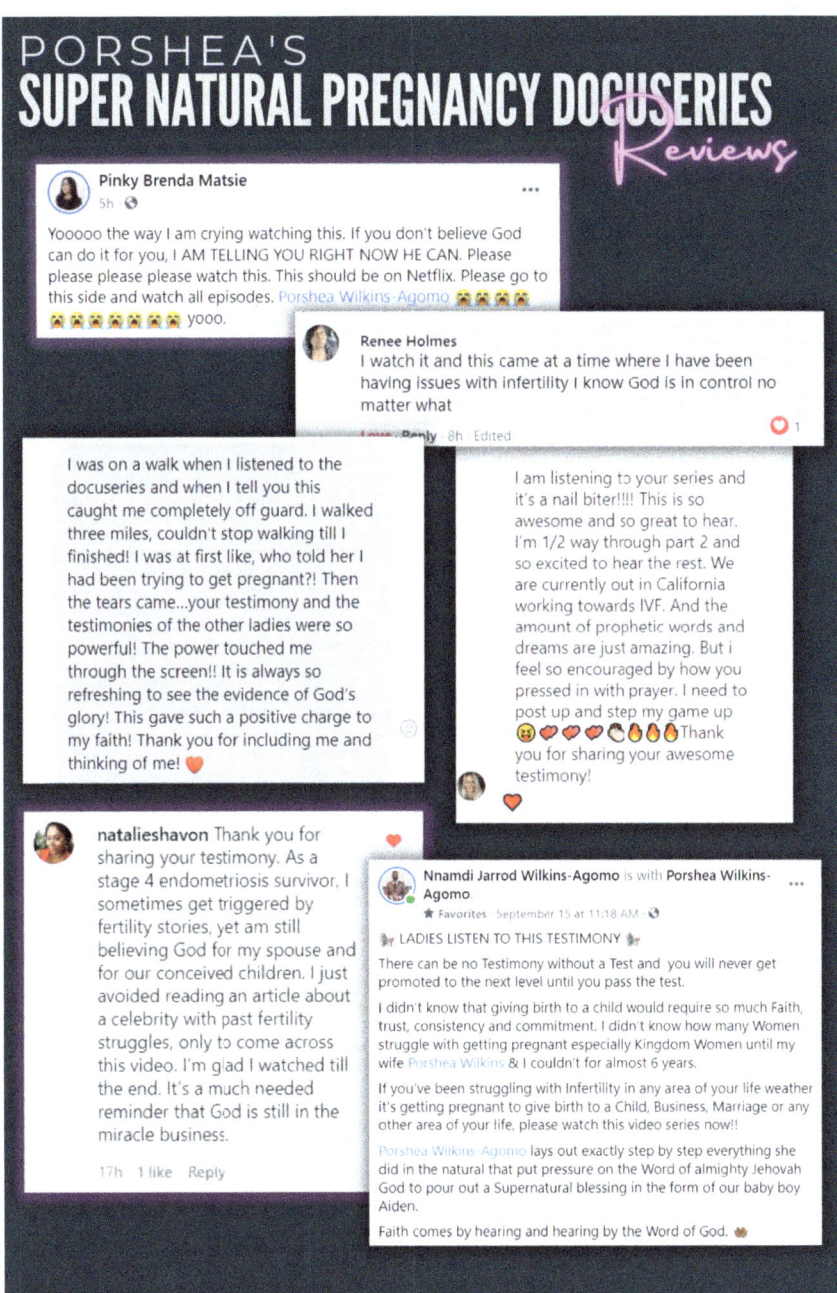

Midwife Moments Podcast

 Available on iTUNES and MidwifeMoments.com